MODERN APPLIQUÉ ILLUSIONS

12 Quilts Create Perspective & Depth

Casey York

stashBOOKS®

an imprint of C&T Publishing

Publisher: Amy Marson

Creative Director: Gailen Runge

Art Director: Kristy Zacharias

Editors: S. Michele Fry and Karla Menaugh

Technical Editors: Alison M. Schmidt and Nanette S. Zeller

Cover/Book Designer: April Mostek

Production Coordinator: Rue Flaherty

Production Editor: Joanna Burgarino

Illustrator: Kirstie L. Petterson

Photo Assistant: Mary Peyton Peppo

Styled photography by Nissa Brehmer and instructional photography by Diane Pedersen, unless otherwise noted

Published by Stash Books, an imprint of C&T Publishing, Inc., P.O. Box 1456, Lafayette, CA 94549

Library of Congress Cataloging-in-Publication Data

York, Casey, 1979-

Modern appliqué illusions : 12 quilts create perspective & depth / Casey York.

    pages cm

ISBN 978-1-60705-925-7 (soft cover)

1. Quilts. 2. Quilting. 3. Appliqué--Patterns. 4. Optical illusions in art. I. Title.

TT835.Y66 2014

746.46--dc23

                    2014013069

Printed in China

10 9 8 7 6 5 4 3 2 1

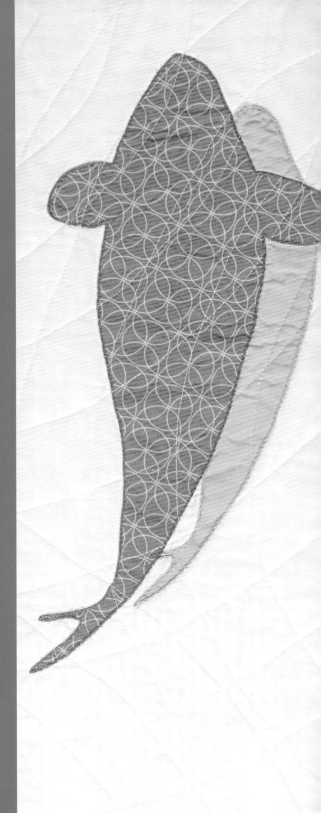

CONTENTS

DEDICATION AND ACKNOWLEDGMENTS 4

INTRODUCTION 6

MATERIALS 9

Fabric • Piecing a Background • Fusible Web • Scissors • Embroidery Supplies

APPLIQUÉ BASICS 13

Using the Patterns • Fusible Web Appliqué • Finishing Raw-Edge Appliqué with Embroidery
Alternative Appliqué Techniques • Hand Stitches

FINISHING THE QUILT 23

Basting • Marking and Quilting • Binding

PROJECTS

ARCHITECTURE 29	**THE NATURAL WORLD 49**	**CONCEPTS 79**
Tunnel Vision 31	River Bend 51	Baby Blocks 81
Concrete Jungle 37	Chicken Scratch 55	Still Life 87
Grand Canal 43	Upward 61	Flight Plan 93
	Grove 67	Perspective 99
	Ripples 73	

RESOURCES 103

ABOUT THE AUTHOR 103

3

DEDICATION

In loving memory of my grandmother, Margaret Gardonio, for her tireless support and boundless enthusiasm, and for always knowing how to motivate me.

ACKNOWLEDGMENTS

This book has been a truly collaborative experience, and many people contributed to bringing it to press. I owe deep thanks to everyone who has participated in the writing and publishing process, as well as to you, my readers. I would like to address special gratitude to the following individuals and companies.

First, many, many thanks to the wonderful editors I have worked with at Stash Books and C&T Publishing. To my developmental editors, Michele Fry and Karla Menaugh, I feel so lucky to have had your guidance and support throughout the development of my manuscript. My technical editor, Alison Schmidt, made sure my instructions were clear and my measurements accurate, ensuring that all of the projects described here would be fun and straightforward to make. My other team members, April Mostek, Nissa Brehmer, Diane Pedersen, Mary Peyton Peppo, Rue Flaherty, Kirstie Petterson, and Joanna Burgarino, translated my scatterbrained design ideas into the beautiful book you hold in your hands, with which I couldn't be happier. To Roxane Cerda and Amy Marson, thank you so much for taking a chance on me and my work, and for your helpful suggestions and encouraging enthusiasm.

I also owe an enormous debt of gratitude to the companies that generously contributed materials to the making of this book and its projects. In no particular order, they include Michael Miller Fabrics, Westminster Fibers/FreeSpirit Fabrics, Spoonflower, The Warm Company, Pellon, Aurifil, and Darice. It has been fantastic working with all of you, and it is my pleasure to recommend your products to my readers.

A huge thank-you goes to Allison Rosen for working with me to chronicle my writing experience online, as well as for her behind-the-scenes advice. Many thanks also to the Stash Books staff and editors who participated in our blogging project.

Many thanks are due my quilters, Angela Walters and Ann McNew, for their beautiful work on several of the quilts in this book. I am in awe of their skill and artistry, and I am so proud to have some of their work represented among the projects here. Thank you also to the staff of Merrily We Sew Along for assisting and encouraging me in my own adventures in longarm quilting. Thank you to Jane, Jenny, and Laurie of Janie Lou for putting up with my incessant visits to their shop and offering sound design advice. Finally, my friends and family have been instrumental in helping me bring the idea of writing a book to fruition. To my husband, Barrett, and our two sons, Julian and Simon, thank you so much for your love, support, and patience during the crazy periods of manuscript preparation. Thank you also to my dad, sisters, and grandma, as well as all of my parents- and siblings-in-law for believing in and encouraging me, and for listening to me prattle on about the writing process. Enduring thanks to my mother for teaching me to sew and instilling a lifelong love of creating. And last but not least, many thanks to the amazing members of the St. Louis Modern Quilt Guild, whose support and encouragement first sparked my interest in writing a book on modern crafting.

INTRODUCTION

"Perspective is a way of thinking about observation, a method that harnesses and organizes space. It is a fundamentally practical technique: given two dimensions, it computes the third and, conversely, permits three dimensions to be projected onto two."

—Pierre Descargues, *Perspective*, 1976

Ever since childhood, I've been fascinated with illusionistic representation. More specifically, I've always been curious about the sleight of hand that allows artists to trick us into seeing three-dimensional space when we're looking at a two-dimensional surface. My first lesson in this trickery was when I was six years old and my dad—using only overlapping lines and strategically placed shadows—taught me to draw ribbons that appeared to curl up off the paper. Fascinated by this newfound skill, I naturally wrote up a how-to-draw book and tried to get my dad to market it to his co-workers. Fast forward to late 2012, when I was inspired by a Modern Quilt Guild fabric challenge and a seventeenth-century painting by Meindert Hobbema—*The Avenue at Middelharnis*—to try to introduce the illusion of depth into a quilt. The result was *Onwards*, a quilt that retains a sense of minimalism while still strongly suggesting a three-dimensional space. I knew the experiment was successful when my two sons responded by trying to "walk into" the quilted perspective. *Onwards* eventually gave rise to the concept for this book, where I've had the remarkable opportunity to explore more fully the concept of using illusionistic representation in the two-dimensional medium of quilting.

The illusion of depth has been a hallmark of Western art since the times of the ancient Greeks and Romans—we humans have always been interested in fooling the eye into believing that flat surfaces are anything but. The story of the ancient Greek painters Zeuxis and Parrhasius illustrates this trait. According to Pliny the Elder,

ONWARDS, 49″ × 51″, made and quilted by Casey York, 2012

Zeuxis and Parrhasius held a contest to see who could create the most convincing illusionistic painting. Zeuxis thought he had won when the grapes he had painted tempted even the birds. However, when he tried to pull back the curtain covering Parrhasius' painting, he realized that it also was painted. Thus, Zeuxis had to grant Parrhasius the victory because the latter's painting had fooled not merely the birds but also a fellow artist.

While they do not attempt to depict the real world in such detail, the quilted projects in this book also achieve the illusion of depth. Most of them do so through a technique called *linear perspective*, which I use often. I'm not alone in using linear perspective. It was invented during the Italian Renaissance and has been used ever since as a way of constructing the illusion of space. Even sculptors and garden designers, whose work actually exists in three dimensions, have used linear perspective to infuse their work with meaning. Entire books have been written about the history of linear perspective and how it works to fool the eye. I've listed a few in Resources (page 103). However, for our purposes, a simple explanation is sufficient.

In linear perspective, parallel lines appear to converge as they recede in space. Theoretically, such lines will eventually meet at a point known as the *vanishing point*, which corresponds to the center of the viewer's field of vision. This technique is known as *one-point perspective*, and it is used in *Onwards* and many of the quilts in this book. A variation, *two-point perspective* (which uses—you guessed it—two vanishing points), allows

oblique views of objects and can be seen in *Concrete Jungle* (page 37).

Another characteristic of perspective is that objects seem to get smaller as they get farther away. At the same time, the ground plane appears to rise to meet the horizon line as the horizon recedes. Accordingly, we can give the impression of three dimensions by placing progressively smaller forms at points progressively closer to the center of the quilt, as in *Chicken Scratch* (page 55) and *Upward* (page 61). On the same principle, many of the quilts in this book use a quilting design of horizontal lines that grow farther apart as they approach the top and bottom of the quilt. You can read more about my method for marking these lines in "Receding" Quilting (page 25).

Finally, the contrast between light and shadow is a powerful indicator of depth. If you adjust the color, value, and texture of different parts of objects, you can trick the eye into thinking an object exists in three dimensions. I use this idea for the hedges in *Grand Canal* (page 43).

The projects in this book explore the potential for using minimal shapes, colors, and compositions to create the illusion of space. I think it's particularly interesting to try to do this on the surface of a quilt, which, by its very nature, is two-dimensional. As I watch my kids use these quilts every day, I am still struck by the artifice of the objects. The illusionistic images catch my eye, briefly fool my brain, and remind me of those artists I admire who aimed to trick the eye.

MATERIALS

Using high-quality supplies and mastering some simple techniques will make creating the projects in this book easier and more enjoyable. This chapter outlines some basic appliqué and quiltmaking techniques, and describes some materials and processes specific to my particular style of appliqué.

Fabric

All the quilts in this book use high-quality quilter's cotton, which is easy to sew by machine and by hand, and comes in an enormous variety of prints and colors. I also enjoy making quilts with other fibers—such as silk and wool—but when I do, I prewash and dry all the fabrics. Fabrics shrink at different rates, and I want all of that shrinkage to take place *before* I stitch those fabrics into a quilt. Although I enjoy the texture produced in cotton quilts by skipping the prewashing step, I prewashed the fabrics for almost all the quilts in this book. The extra step was worth it in order to ensure that no colors bled onto white backgrounds and no fabrics shrank unevenly.

Most quilting cotton is available in bolts 44″ to 45″ wide. However, it is safer to assume a width of 40″ because of the differences in the widths of selvages and in degree of shrinkage, as well as possible printing and cutting imperfections.

Many of the quilts in this book have white backgrounds, and I prefer to use extra-wide premium muslin for this purpose. Robert Kaufman makes premium muslin that comes up to 118″ wide, available in natural and bleached white, which is my favorite base cloth because of its high thread count and soft hand. The extra width allows me to avoid having seams running across my backgrounds. If you find yourself using narrower fabric, however, follow the instructions in Piecing a Background (page 10).

PIECING A BACKGROUND

When possible, I approach piecing a background using methods borrowed from piecing large quilt backings. It is best to avoid having seams along the central axes of the quilt in order to reduce potential stress on the seams when the quilt is folded.

1 If possible, orient seams parallel to the longest edge of the quilt top. You will need enough fabric to equal twice the length of the longest quilt dimension. All of the projects in this book include material requirements for both pieced and wholecloth quilt backgrounds, so the yardage requirements have already been calculated for you.

2 To orient the seams parallel to the long edge of the quilt, cut the yardage to equal the long edge of the quilt. For example, if you are making a quilt that measures 80″ long by 60″ wide, cut the yardage into 80″-long sections. **FIGURE A**

3 Cut one of the sections in half lengthwise. For instance, if making the quilt example in Step 2, cut an 80″ section into 2 sections 20″ × 80″. **FIGURE B**

4 Using a ¼″ seam allowance, stitch the 20″ sections to either side of the remaining 40″ section, matching 80″ edges. Press seams open. **FIGURE C**

5 Cut the resulting panel of fabric to measure 60″ × 80″. **FIGURE D**

A

B

C

D

Fusible Web

The projects in this book are simple to put together because they use double-sided lightweight fusible web. This product allows you to trace appliqué patterns onto the transparent fusible material and then transfer those tracings directly onto the wrong side of your fabrics for cutting. After you have cut out the appliqués, they can be fused to the background material in preparation for stitching.

There are many brands and weights of fusible web. It is important to buy the lightest weight available in your chosen brand, because heavier weights can add stiffness and bulk to your quilts. My favorite is Pellon's regular-weight 805 Wonder-Under. This product includes a single-paper backing, making tracing patterns straightforward. It also fuses quickly and easily to fabrics without adding stiffness. If you want to wash your quilt, you will need to stitch the appliqués to the background to secure them, and Wonder-Under can be sewn with your machine or by hand.

Scissors

The paper backing on fusible web dulls scissor blades quickly. I have separate pairs of scissors dedicated to cutting the web alone (and other paper), the web once it is fused to my fabrics, and fabric alone. This lets me avoid having the blades of my fabric-dedicated scissors dulled or gummed up by cutting the fusible web. If you choose to use embroidery to finish your appliqué edges, I recommend also investing in a pair of small embroidery scissors, which are invaluable for clipping small threads close to the surface of the fabric.

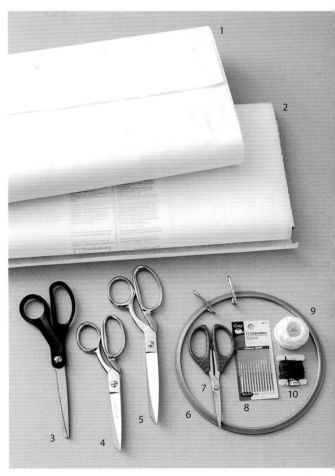

Supplies you'll need:

1. 118″-wide premium muslin
2. lightweight fusible web
3. paper scissors
4. appliqué scissors
5. fabric scissors
6. spring-tension embroidery hoop
7. embroidery scissors
8. embroidery needles
9. perle cotton
10. embroidery floss

Embroidery Supplies

If you choose to finish your appliqué edges with embroidery, you will need special materials.

First, invest in high-quality thread for embroidery, such as embroidery floss or perle cotton. I usually use three strands of six-stranded cotton embroidery floss, but many types of embroidery thread are available, so experiment to learn what works best for you and your projects.

You also will want an embroidery hoop to hold your fabric taut while you work the stitches. These come in various sizes and shapes. I favor Darice spring-tension hoops, which make it easy to reposition quilt tops and to adjust the tension as I am stitching.

Finally, invest in some dedicated embroidery needles. These have longer eyes than regular hand-sewing needles, making it easier to thread multiple strands of embroidery floss.

TIP The eyes of most needles are punched through the metal, so the surface of the eye is smoother on one side of the needle than it is on the other. If you are having trouble threading your needle, try threading it from the other side.

For the basic stitches required for the projects in this book, see Hand Stitches (page 21).

APPLIQUÉ BASICS

Using the Patterns

The appliqué patterns in this book are available at tinyurl.com/11067-patterns-download so that you can download a zipped file, save it to your computer, and then print the PDF files as needed from your home computer or send them to a copy center. The patterns are full size, so you won't have to worry about having them enlarged. The PDF files are designed to be printed on standard 8½″ × 11″ paper, with a diagram showing how to assemble the larger patterns from the printouts.

The PDFs can be opened in most PDF-reader software programs. If you don't have one already, you can download Adobe Reader for free from adobe.com. This program is recommended because it will give you the most printing and scaling options. Printing directly from your browser is not recommended, as it can alter the print size.

Open the PDF file of the quilt you are making. Refer to the pattern piece names and schematics to choose some or all of the patterns for the appliqués. Make sure to select the software's "Actual Size" or "Print at 100%" option, if available.

Before printing all the pages, you may want to print a single page and measure the 1″ crosshairs to check whether the pattern has printed at the correct size. If it has, you are good to go.

After all the pages are printed, follow the schematic on the pages to tape them together to assemble the entire pattern.

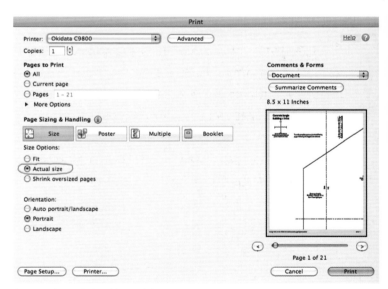
Screenshot of the "Actual Size" option

One final note about the patterns: They are reversed for tracing onto fusible web. If you choose an alternative method of appliqué, trace the patterns directly onto the *wrong* side of the fabric. The patterns do not include seam allowances for turned-edge appliqué; if you use this method, add approximately ¼″ around each shape.

Fusible Web Appliqué

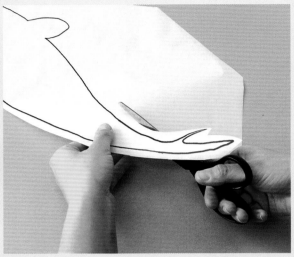

A Trace the pattern onto the paper side of the web.   **B** Cut the traced pattern from the web.

The projects will come together quickly if you use fusible web to secure the appliqués to the background fabric. For projects that will be washed, you should also stitch around each appliqué.

Remember to refer to the manufacturer's directions for the brand of web you use. Different types of web require different iron settings to adhere to fabric correctly.

1 Transfer your design onto the fusible web. Most webs have a paper backing, so just lay the fusible web over your printout and trace your pattern onto the paper backing. Since fusible web has no grain, you can rotate the patterns as needed to fit tightly together and waste as little web as possible. **FIGURE A**

2 Roughly cut the pattern from the fusible web, leaving a ¼˝ margin outside the traced line. **FIGURE B**

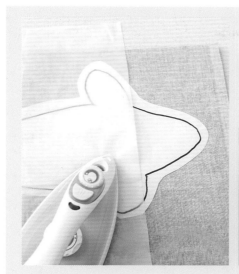 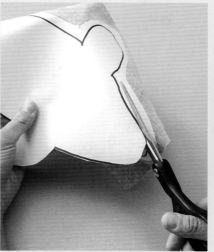 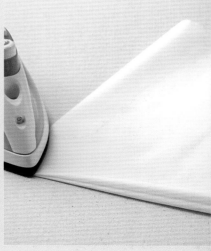

C Fuse the web to the wrong side of the appliqué fabric.

D Cut the appliqué on the traced line.

E Fold and crease the background fabric.

3 Place the traced pattern, paper side up, on the wrong side of the appliqué fabric. Use an iron to fuse it to the fabric. Use an appliqué pressing sheet or Silicone Release Paper (from C&T Publishing) to protect your iron from any fusible residue. **FIGURE C**

4 Cut out the appliqué along the traced lines. **FIGURE D**

5 Lay out your background fabric and make any reference marks listed in the instructions. Usually I fold the background in half vertically and horizontally to find the center and press the folds to make creased lines. **FIGURE E**

F Peel off the backing.

G Pin the appliqués in place.

H Remove the pins and fuse in place.

6 Remove the paper backing from the appliqués and position them on the background, referring to the project's placement diagram. **FIGURE F**

7 When you are satisfied with the appliqué placement, pin the shapes in place. (Even if it is slightly sticky, the fusible web will not hold the appliqués in place accurately when you move the quilt top.) **FIGURE G**

8 Following the manufacturer's directions, use an iron to fuse the appliqués to the background, removing pins before you fuse each section. You don't need to fuse just one appliqué at a time; I often fuse several (or portions of several) at the same time if they are close together. This helps preserve the placement of the appliqués relative to one another. Project instructions include notes if certain appliqués are to be fused first or separately. **FIGURE H**

I Zigzag stitching along a straight edge

J Zigzag stitching around a curve

K Pivot to zigzag stitch around a corner.

9 Stitch around each appliqué by machine or by hand. If you use the machine, you can use a zigzag stitch, catching the appliqué on the inside of the zigzag and the background fabric on the outside, and making sure to catch the appliqué with each stitch. A machine blanket stitch will also work well for sewing down the appliqués. I use a clear plastic open-toe appliqué presser foot, which allows me to see my line of stitching and make sure I am consistently catching the appliqué fabric. To round a curve or corner, stop with the needle down on the outside of the appliqué and raise the presser foot to pivot the fabric. **FIGURES I, J, & K**

I use clear nylon thread to stitch around my appliqués, which renders the stitches invisible. Because the stitches are invisible, I lock my stitches by overlapping the stitches as I finish sewing around each appliqué. I backstitch a couple stitches on appliqués that do not require stitching all the way around the perimeter (such as the hedges in *Grand Canal*, page 43). If you choose to use non-invisible thread to sew down your appliqués, you can avoid visible overlapping stitches or backstitches by pulling both the top and bottom threads to the back of the quilt top and tying off to secure.

If you choose to hand stitch the fusible appliqués to your quilt top as opposed to sewing on a machine, I recommend using a blanket stitch (page 21) and matching thread.

A Mark the pattern at the edge of the web.

B Line up the web at the pattern marking and continue tracing.

- Some large patterns may not fit on a single piece of web, so you will have to trace the pattern onto multiple pieces to be reassembled when you fuse the web to the appliqué fabric. To do this, trace a section of the pattern, marking the pattern where it meets the edges of the web. Line up a second piece of web with the line you made on your pattern and continue tracing the shape. **FIGURES A & B**

- Some brands of web have two paper backings. If you use this type of web, take special care to trace the pattern onto the paper that *does not* peel away from the web easily; otherwise, you will remove your tracing with the first paper backing when you fuse the web to the appliqué fabric.

- If the traced pattern is large, you can cut out the center of the web to reduce stiffness in the finished quilt. To do this, cut along the inside of the pattern contours, about $1/2''$ from the traced line. You will be left with a fusible "outline." **FIGURE C**

- Use an appliqué pressing sheet or Silicone Release Paper (from C&T Publishing) to protect your iron from the fusible adhesive.

- It is helpful to find the center point of the background fabric before placing appliqués. To do this, fold the fabric in half vertically and horizontally; the place where the two creases meet is the center point. **FIGURE D**

C Remove the web from the center of the appliqué before fusing to reduce stiffness in the finished quilt.

D Find the center by folding in both directions.

- For many designs, it is easiest to place the central appliqué first and use it as a reference point for placing the remaining appliqués. For other designs, it is easier to start with the appliqué closest to one edge and move across the background to the opposite side. You will find specific directions for placing the appliqués with the instructions for each project.

- Stand back from your quilt top occasionally—this will help you see any adjustments that need to be made in the appliqué layout.

- Minimal pinning is necessary with fusible web appliqué. I usually use a couple pins to anchor my pieces in place so they don't shift position when I move the background fabric to the ironing board. If the appliqués move during this process, you can easily reposition them when you smooth the fabric onto the ironing surface.

- To create a clean edge on your appliqués, use a clear, or "invisible," nylon thread. With the invisible thread on top, use a regular cotton thread in the bobbin to reduce tangles and snags. I use a bobbin thread that matches my background fabric. Make sure to test your machine's tension on the fabrics you plan to use and make any necessary adjustments. Different sewing machines handle different brands and weights of nylon thread differently, so you may also want to experiment with a couple different threads if your machine gives you trouble. I have found Aurifil invisible nylon thread to give the best results with most machines.

Finishing Raw-Edge Appliqué with Embroidery

If you wash raw-edge appliqué, the edges of the fabric will fray slightly. Sometimes this effect is desirable, but I usually prefer that my appliqués retain clean, finished edges. To finish the edges, I outline the appliqués with a hand-embroidered chain stitch (page 21) over the top of my zigzag stitching to encase the raw edges.

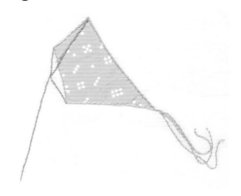

If you want your outlines to stand out, use a thread that contrasts with the appliqué fabric. Otherwise, match the threads carefully to the appliqué fabrics.

TIP The best way to determine if a thread matches the appliqué fabric is to look at both together in natural light. Because this can be difficult when shopping for thread, I often buy a couple of different colors and compare them with my quilt top later before deciding which color to use. When an exact match is not possible and I have to choose between two imperfectly matching colors, I find that erring on the side of the lighter color gives the most unobtrusive results.

Alternative Appliqué Techniques

Although I find raw-edge appliqué to work best for intricate shapes, the projects in this book also can be made using other appliqué techniques. These include turned-edge techniques, in which the edges of each appliqué are turned under. Some turned-edge techniques use freezer paper, interfacing, or other materials to help turn the edges of the appliqué pieces before they are applied to the background. Alternatively, with needle-turn appliqué, the edges are turned under with the needle as the appliqué is hand stitched to the background. Abundant resources exist on these techniques, both in print and on the Internet. *If you choose to use a turned-edge method of appliqué for the projects in this book, remember to add your desired seam allowance when tracing the patterns and to trace the patterns onto the wrong side of the appliqué fabric.*

Hand Stitches

BLANKET STITCH

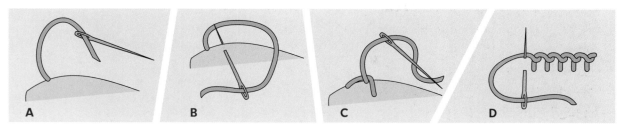

1 Bring the needle to the right side of the fabric adjacent to the appliqué.
FIGURE A

2 Insert the needle about ¼˝ to the right and about ¼˝ in from the edge of the appliqué fabric. Do not pull the thread all the way through. **FIGURE B**

3 Bring the needle back up about ¼˝ to the right of the first stitch, catching the loop of thread. **FIGURE C**

4 Pull the thread taut, creating a right angle. Repeat along the contours of the appliqué. **FIGURE D**

CHAIN STITCH

1 Bring the needle to the right side of the fabric and pull the thread through (A). **FIGURE A**

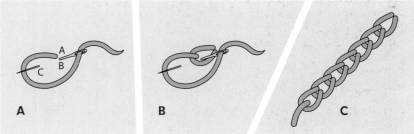

2 Insert the needle into the same hole through which it came up or close by (B). Pull the thread to the wrong side of the fabric, leaving a loop of thread on the right side. **FIGURE A**

3 Bring the needle back to the right side of the fabric about ¼˝ away, inserting it through the loop of thread, and pull taut (C). **FIGURE A**

4 Repeat along the contours of the appliqué. Finish by making a straight stitch over the last loop of thread. **FIGURES B & C**

STEM STITCH

1 Bring the needle to the right side of the fabric and pull the thread through (A). **FIGURE A**

2 Insert the needle into the fabric about ¼″ away (B); do not pull the thread all the way through. **FIGURE A**

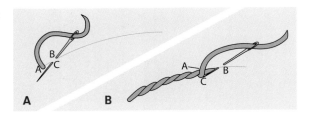

3 Bring the needle back to the right side of the fabric (C) halfway between A and B; pull the thread taut. **FIGURE A**

4 Repeat Steps 2 and 3, this time bringing the needle back up at the point where the last stitch finished. **FIGURE B**

BACKSTITCH

1 Bring the needle to the right side of the fabric and pull the thread through (A). Insert the needle into the fabric ¼″ away and complete a single stitch (B). **FIGURE A**

2 Bring the needle to the right side of the fabric about ¼″ from the point where the last stitch ended (C); pull the thread through. **FIGURE B**

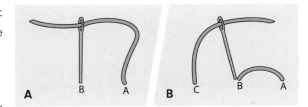

3 Insert the needle into the fabric at the point where the last stitch ended (B); pull the thread through. **FIGURE B**

4 Repeat Steps 2 and 3.

FRENCH KNOT

1 Bring the needle to the right side of the fabric and pull the thread through (A). **FIGURE A**

2 Wrap the thread around the needle two or three times, and insert the needle back into the same hole (B). **FIGURES A & B**

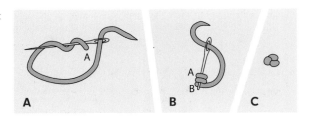

3 Keeping the wrapped thread taut against the needle, pull the thread through to the wrong side of the fabric. **FIGURE C**

FINISHING THE QUILT

To finish your quilt, cut the backing fabric and batting to measure 4″ larger than the quilt measurements on each side (a total of 8″ larger than the final quilt measurements). For smaller quilts such as *Still Life* (page 87), the backing and batting can be cut a total of 4″ larger. Piece the backing with ¼″ seams if needed to make it the required size. I prefer to orient my backing seams parallel to the longest edge of the quilt, but orienting seams parallel to the shorter edge may require less yardage than listed.

On a large, flat surface, layer the quilt backing (right side down), the batting, and the quilt top (right side up), centering the quilt top on the lower layers and carefully smoothing out any wrinkles. I usually complete this step on a carpeted surface, which reduces shifting of my backing fabric. If you do this step on a smooth surface, such as a hard floor, you may find it helpful to anchor the backing fabric to the surface with painter's tape.

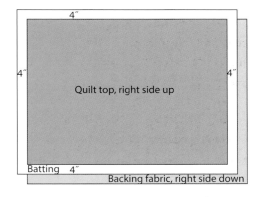

Basting

Note: I prefer to mark my quilting lines as I am quilting, after basting the quilt. If you would prefer to mark your quilt top before basting, refer to Marking and Quilting (page 24) before making the quilt sandwich.

When all three layers are smooth, baste the quilt sandwich. There are a number of options:

■ Thread basting is done by hand using a contrasting thread and a running stitch. Begin in the center of the quilt and baste toward the outer edges, smoothing any wrinkles that form as you stitch. Make your stitches about 1″–2″ long and leave about 1″–2″ between rows of stitches. Using a contrasting thread will make your stitches easy to see for removal after quilting.

- Many quilters prefer pin basting. Place the pins about 4″ apart over the entire surface of the quilt, starting in the center and moving toward the outer edges. Remove the pins as you quilt. When I remove my pins, I like to leave them open so that they are ready for my next basting project.

- Spray basting is another option. In this method, an aerosol adhesive is applied between each layer to temporarily glue the layers together for quilting. After quilting, most basting sprays wash out. If you choose to spray baste your quilt, follow the manufacturer's directions for your basting spray product.

Marking and Quilting

Many of the projects in this book use the quilting design to suggest or enhance the illusion of depth. For these quilts, the suggested quilting pattern is in the project instructions. These quilting patterns utilize straight-line quilting, and they should be easy to complete on a home sewing machine. Use a walking foot to help all layers of the quilt move through the machine at the same speed, minimizing tucks and creases in the layers. For best results, do not quilt over appliqués (unless it is directed in the project instructions, as in *Ripples*, page 73). Stop quilting at one edge of the appliqué and pick up the line on the other, making sure to either lock your stitches or leave thread tails for tying off on either side of the appliqué.

Marking tools:

1. mechanical chalk pencil
2. Hera marker
3. water-soluble pencil
4. water-soluble pens
5. chalk

Straight-line quilting is easier if you mark the quilting lines; you can then follow along these lines as you sew. Many tools exist for marking quilts, including tailor's chalk, water-soluble markers, and markers that disappear when heat is applied. Painter's or masking tape also works well for marking straight lines; just be careful not to leave tape on your quilt top for extended periods to avoid having the adhesive leave residue. One of my favorite tools for straight-line quilting is a Hera marker, which marks by creating a crease in the fabric instead of applying a pigment to its surface. I find that Hera markers work especially well on sandwiched quilts, where the crease is accentuated by the additional depth of the batting.

After quilting, trim the batting and backing flush with the quilt top, and remove any remaining basting pins or threads.

"RECEDING" QUILTING

In several quilts, I quilted horizontal lines to create the appearance of a receding ground plane. My technique for marking these lines is outlined below.

1 Find the horizon line in your quilt layout. Often you will have marked this line with a crease when you arranged the appliqués. Receding quilting can be used both below this line, to represent the ground plane, and above it, to represent the sky.

2 Measure ½˝ away from this line and mark another horizontal line, parallel to the horizon line. This is your first line of quilting.

3 For each subsequent line of quilting, add ½˝ to the previous measurement. So, for the second line of quilting, measure 1˝ away from the first, for the third line of quilting, measure 1½˝ away from the second, and so on.

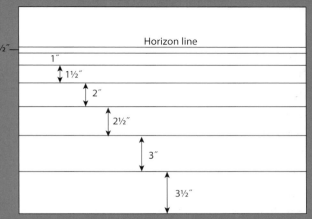

Spacing quilting lines

4 Continue until you reach the edge of the quilt top.

5 For best results, do not quilt over any appliqués. Stop quilting at one edge of the appliqué and pick up the line on the other. Make sure to either lock your quilting stitches or leave long thread tails to tie off and bury on either side of each appliqué.

6 Quilting wavy lines can produce a more organic appearance. The process for measuring and marking the lines remains the same. To quilt a wavy line, allow your quilted line to move slightly above and below the marked line to produce waves.

Binding

Just as there are multiple appliqué methods, there are many different ways to make and apply binding to a quilt, and everybody has a favorite. I prefer hand-finished double-fold bias binding—I find that it gives me the smoothest finish and the best mitered corners. I also prefer the look of wider bindings as frames for my quilts, so I tend to cut my bindings a little wider than others do (3″-wide strips, as compared with 2½″ strips). Feel free to follow these instructions or use your own favorite binding method. Please note, however, that quilts with curved edges (*Grand Canal*, page 45; *Chicken Scratch*, page 55; and *Baby Blocks*, page 81) *must* use binding cut on the bias to ease around their curves.

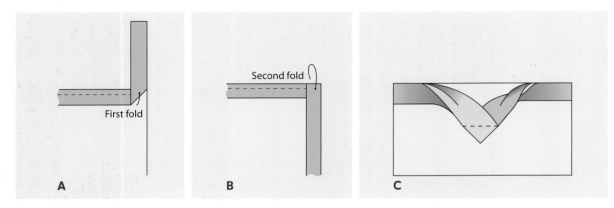

1 Beginning at least 15″ from any corner of the trimmed quilt, pin the binding to the front of the quilt so that all raw edges align. Pin until you reach the first corner. Begin stitching at least 12″ from the end of the binding. (The free tail of binding will be necessary when you join the binding strips in Step 5.)

2 Using a ⅜″ seam allowance, stitch along the pinned length, stopping ⅜″ from the edge of the quilt. Backstitch. This wider seam allowance is what creates the wider finished binding that I prefer.

3 Fold the binding up so that the fold forms a 45° angle in the corner, and press. Fold the binding back down upon itself, parallel to the next edge of the quilt to be sewn; press. **FIGURES A & B**

4 Repeat Steps 2 and 3 for the remaining edges of the quilt. Stop stitching at least 12″ from your starting point.

5 To finish the binding, bring the two ends together and overlap them. Trim the ends so that they overlap by 3″ (or the width of your unfolded binding). Unfold the binding and align the cut edges at a 90° angle, right sides together. Stitch on the diagonal, trim to a ¼″ seam allowance, and press the seam. **FIGURE C**

6 Refold the binding, press, and align the raw edges with the raw edges of the quilt; pin in place and stitch.

7 To finish the back, fold the binding around the ⅜″ seam allowance to the back of the quilt and stitch in place by hand.

MAKING BIAS BINDING

Method 1

1 Square up your fabric to be sure the vertical and horizontal edges are on grain. Align your ruler so that the 45° line is parallel to the squared-up edge; cut along the length of the ruler. **FIGURE 1A**

2 Working parallel to the 45° cut you just made, cut 3″-wide strips. **FIGURE 1B**

3 Align the ends of the strips as shown in the diagram and stitch together, creating one long strip of fabric. Trim the dog-ears, leaving a ¼″ seam allowance. **FIGURE 1C**

4 Fold the strip in half lengthwise, *wrong* sides together, and press.

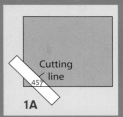
1A

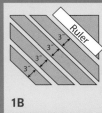
1B

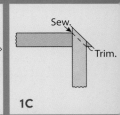
1C

Method 2—Continuous Bias Binding

Making continuous bias binding involves using a square sliced in half diagonally, and then sewing the resulting triangles together. You then mark strips, sew again to make a tube, and cut to make a continuous binding strip of the desired length.

1 Cut the fabric for the bias binding so it is a square. For example, if yardage is ½ yard, cut an 18″ × 18″ square.

2 Cut the square in half diagonally, creating 2 triangles. Using a ¼″ seam, sew the triangles together as shown; press the seam open. **FIGURE 2A**

3 Using a ruler, mark the resulting parallelogram with lines spaced the width of your binding strips (for example, 3″ to make the extra-wide binding I prefer). Cut about 5″ along the first line, as shown. **FIGURE 2B**

4 Join Side 1 and Side 2 to form a tube. The raw edge at point A will align with the raw edge at point B, allowing the first line to be offset by one strip width. With right sides together, pin the raw edges, making sure that the marked lines match up. Sew with a ¼″ seam allowance; press the seam open.

5 Cut along the drawn lines, creating one continuous strip. **FIGURE 2C**

6 Fold the entire strip in half lengthwise, *wrong* sides together, and press.

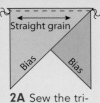
2A Sew the triangles together to form a parallelogram.

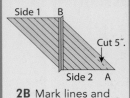
2B Mark lines and begin cutting the first line.

2C Cut along the drawn lines.

"Our perceptions of size and distance are interrelated—we cannot accurately gauge the size of an object without knowing how far away it is, and vice versa."

—E. H. Gombrich,
Art and Illusion, 1960

28

Different cultures have devised different methods of representing depth. Some forms of linear perspective show receding lines running parallel to one another or diverging. Before the seventeenth century, Chinese and Japanese artists often represented space using a sophisticated system of parallel diagonal lines to represent receding forms.

Architecture

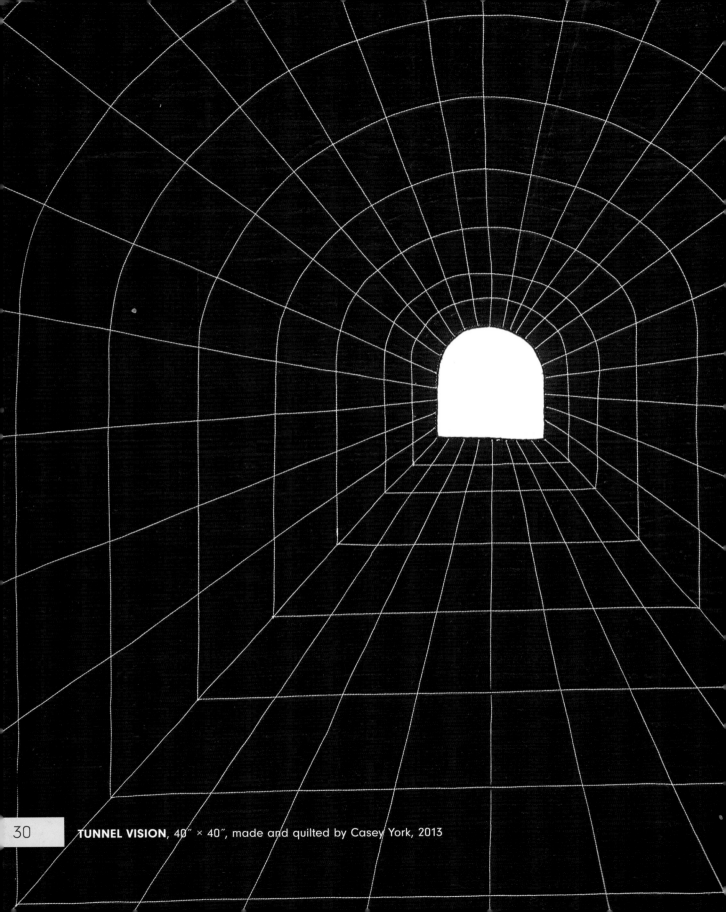

TUNNEL VISION, 40˝ × 40˝, made and quilted by Casey York, 2013

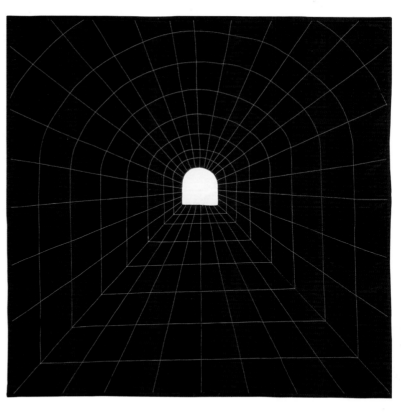

TUNNEL VISION

FINISHED SIZE: 40″ × 40″

The simplest of reverse appliqué combines with radiating quilting lines in contrasting thread to create the illusion of depth in this minimal, yet evocative, quilt. While the reverse appliqué is a little different from the appliqué in most of the projects in this book, it is just as easy. Although these instructions are for a small quilt, this pattern could easily be adapted for a larger size. Simply enlarge the appliqué pattern and background measurements to the desired size.

materials

Unless otherwise noted, all measurements refer to 40″-wide, 100% cotton quilting fabric.

NAVY: 1½ yards for background

WHITE: ¼ yard or 1 fat quarter for the light at the end of the tunnel

BACKING: 3 yards

BATTING: 48″ × 48″

BINDING: 1 yard for bias binding or ½ yard for straight-grain binding

LIGHTWEIGHT FUSIBLE WEB, 15″ WIDE: ¼ yard

EMBROIDERY FLOSS (optional): 1 skein to match background fabric

Assembling the Quilt Top

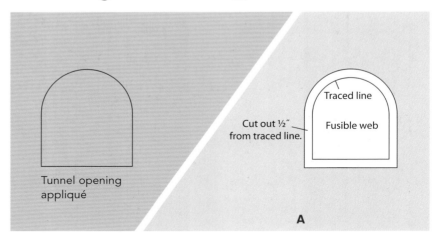

Tunnel opening appliqué

Traced line

Cut out ½″ from traced line.

Fusible web

A

Refer to Appliqué Basics (pages 13–22) for details about printing the patterns and using the techniques needed for this project. *The appliqué patterns do not require any seam allowance. Use a ¼″ seam allowance for piecing, unless otherwise stated.*

1 Cut background fabric to measure 40″ × 40″.

2 Print the *Tunnel Vision* appliqué pattern (page PDF1-1) and trace onto fusible web. Cut out the shape, leaving a ½″ allowance *outside* the traced lines. **FIGURE A**

3 Prepare the background fabric by folding it in half horizontally and vertically, pressing the folds in both directions. The horizontal line will be a placement line for the appliqué, and the vertical line will help with placement of quilting lines.

4 On the *wrong* side of the background fabric, center the fusible-web shape and line up the bottom traced line with the horizontal center line of the background. Fuse to the *wrong* side of the background fabric. **FIGURE B**

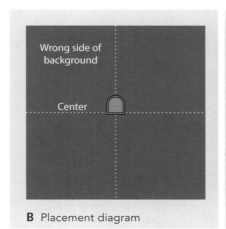

Wrong side of background

Center

B Placement diagram

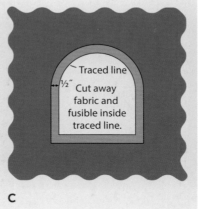

Traced line

½"

Cut away fabric and fusible inside traced line.

C

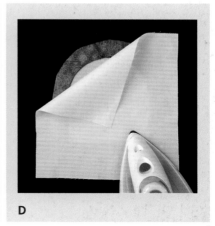

D

TIP In reverse appliqué, a contrasting fabric is appliquéd behind the background fabric. The fusible web is applied to the wrong side of the background fabric, and the smaller, contrasting appliqué fabric is positioned underneath. If it is easier, think of it as fusing a very large appliqué (the background fabric) onto a much smaller contrasting background (the white light at the end of the tunnel).

5 Cut out the *inside* of the web's appliqué shape along the traced line.
FIGURE C

6 Cut a square 6˝ × 6˝ from the white fabric.

7 With the background fabric right side down, position the white fabric square, also right side down, so that it completely covers the cutout and the fusible on the background. Following the manufacturer's instructions, fuse the reverse appliqué piece in place. **FIGURE D**

8 On the right side of the fabric, stitch the background to the reverse appliqué. Carefully trim excess white fabric from the wrong side of the quilt top, close to the stitching line. If you wish, embroider around the appliqué on the right side of the quilt top (refer to Finishing Raw Edge Appliqué with Embroidery, page 20).

Finishing

For more information about basting, marking, quilting, and binding your quilt, see Finishing the Quilt (page 23).

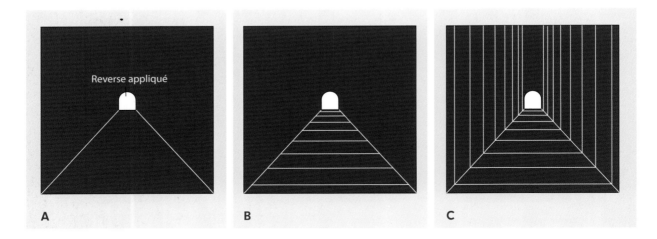

A   **B**   **C**

QUILTING

1 Layer the quilt top, batting, and backing; baste.

2 Using a removable marker, draw diagonal lines from the lower corners of the tunnel appliqué to the corresponding lower corners of the background. **FIGURE A**

3 Mark horizontal quilting lines between the 2 diagonal lines you just marked, starting ½˝ below the bottom of the appliqué. Space lines progressively farther apart. Refer to "Receding" Quilting (page 25). **FIGURE B**

4 Mark arched quilting lines from the tunnel opening outward:

a. From each intersection of a horizontal line with the initial diagonal guidelines, mark a vertical line to the top of the quilt on both sides of the tunnel opening. **FIGURE C**

b. Measure the distance between the edge of the tunnel opening appliqué and the vertical line closest to it. This

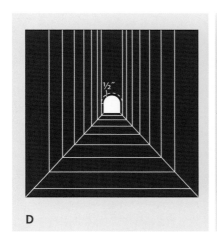

D

E

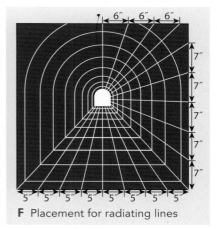

F Placement for radiating lines

measurement determines the distance of the first arched quilting line above the tunnel opening. **FIGURE D**

c. Use this measurement to make a series of tick marks around the curved top of the tunnel opening, and then connect them to form an arch that meets the vertical lines on both sides of the tunnel opening. After you have drawn each arch, you can disregard or erase the vertical lines above it. **FIGURE D**

d. Measure the distance between the first and second vertical lines. Use this measurement to mark and draw a second arch above the first. Work from the center outward to continue measuring and marking arches. **FIGURE E**

5 Following the placement diagram, mark a series of lines radiating from the center of the tunnel appliqué. **FIGURE F**

6 Using a walking foot, quilt along the marked lines with a contrasting thread.

BINDING

1 Trim the batting and backing flush with the quilt top.

2 Refer to Making Bias Binding (page 27) to make the binding, or use your favorite method.

3 Bind the quilt.

CONCRETE JUNGLE, 53″ × 70″, made and quilted by Casey York, 2013

CONCRETE JUNGLE

FINISHED SIZE: 53″ × 70″

Although most of the quilts in this book use one-point perspective, *Concrete Jungle* uses two-point perspective to create the illusion of a row of buildings extending into the distance. The large size of the appliqués makes this an advanced quilt to tackle, but the striking illusion of light and shadow on three-dimensional forms is worth it.

materials

Unless otherwise noted, all measurements refer to 40˝-wide, 100% cotton quilting fabric. • This quilt features the Parson Gray World Tour collection by David Butler for FreeSpirit Fabrics.

WHITE PREMIUM MUSLIN: 1⅝ yards 90˝ or wider for background, or 4⅛ yards for pieced background

LIGHT GRAY: 1¾ yards for Building 1 Front

DARK GRAY: 1¾ yards for Building 1 Side

MEDIUM GRAY OR BLUE: 1⅓ yards for Building 2 Front

DARK GRAY OR BLUE: 1⅓ yards for Building 2 Side

BEIGE: 1⅓ yards for Building 3 Front

GOLD: 1⅓ yards for Building 3 Side

LIGHT BEIGE: ⅓ yard for Building 4 Front

MEDIUM OR DARK BEIGE: ⅛ yard for Building 4 Side

LIGHT RUST: ⅛ yard for Building 5 Front

DARK RUST: ¼ yard for Building 5 Side

BEIGE OR LIGHT BROWN: ⅛ yard for Building 6 Front

MEDIUM OR DARK BROWN: ¼ yard for Building 6 Side

BACKING: 4½ yards for pieced backing

BATTING: 61˝ × 78˝

BINDING: 1 yard for bias binding or ⅔ yard for straight-grain binding

LIGHTWEIGHT FUSIBLE WEB, 15˝ WIDE: 8 yards

EMBROIDERY FLOSS (*optional*): 1 skein to match each appliqué fabric

TIP Some of the appliqués for this quilt are almost 5´ long, which makes it challenging to work with the fusible web and fabric. Go slowly, and give yourself plenty of room to arrange your materials. Don't get discouraged—the results will be worth it!

Assembling the Quilt Top

Refer to Appliqué Basics (pages 13–22) for details about printing the patterns and using the techniques needed for this project. *The appliqué patterns do not require any seam allowance. Use a ¼˝ seam allowance for piecing, unless otherwise stated.*

1 Prepare the *Concrete Jungle* appliqués (pages PDF2-1–PDF2-68). Refer to the materials list to determine the appliqué shapes to cut from each fabric. To reduce bulk, cut out the center of the fusible web from the large patterns before fusing the web to the wrong side of the appliqué fabric. **Note:** The dashed lines on some of the appliqué patterns indicate places where the appliqué will need to be tucked under an overlapping piece; trace and cut on the solid outer line.

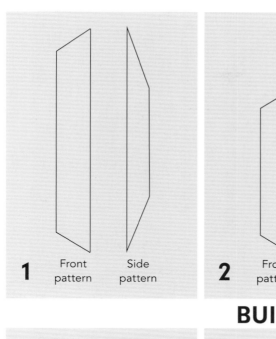

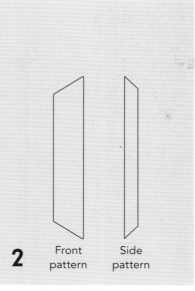

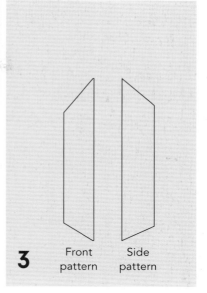

1   Front pattern   Side pattern

2   Front pattern   Side pattern

3   Front pattern   Side pattern

BUILDINGS

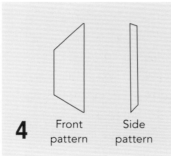

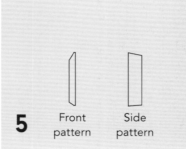

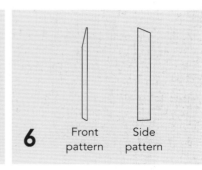

4   Front pattern   Side pattern

5   Front pattern   Side pattern

6   Front pattern   Side pattern

TIP Be especially careful to keep the long edges of the fusible web pieces parallel to one another as you fuse them to the appliqué fabric. Begin fusing at a corner and work along the long edge first; then fuse the short edge, and then the second long edge.

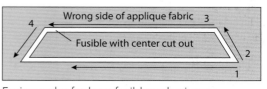

Fusing order for long fusible web pieces

2   Cut or piece background fabric to measure 53″ × 70″.

3   With the background fabric oriented lengthwise, place the appliqué for Building 1 Side along the left side of the fabric, about 2½″ in, and centered from top to bottom. Place the Building 1 Front appliqué to the right of Building 1 Side, tucking the extra ¼″ of fabric on the building front under the building side piece. **FIGURE A (PAGE 40)**

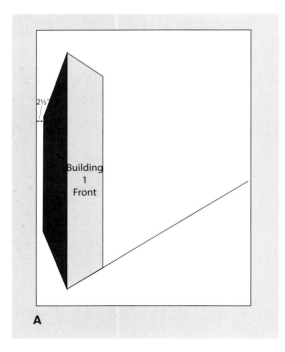

A

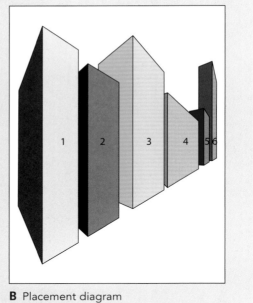

B Placement diagram

4 Using a long ruler or straightedge, extend the baseline of Building 1 Front to the right-hand edge of the background fabric, and mark it. This line will guide you in lining up the rest of the appliqués. **FIGURE A**

5 Following the placement diagram and working from left to right, repeat Step 3 to arrange the remaining appliqués along the baseline, and pin in place. **FIGURE B**

6 Trim the points at the tops and bottoms of the building front appliqués that extend beyond the sides, so that they meet perfectly at the corners. **FIGURE C**

7 Tuck each building side under the building front to its left. Carefully cut away the extra fabric from the building side appliqués that is covered by the building front appliqués, making sure to leave enough to tuck under at least ¼″. **FIGURE D**

TIP Trimming the appliqués as they are placed and pinned to the background, instead of when they are first cut from the web, ensures that edges will match perfectly.

8 When you are satisfied with the layout, fuse the appliqués in place.

C Trim building front points when they extend beyond the building sides.

D Trim the left-hand edge of the building sides, leaving a ¼˝ margin to tuck under the adjacent building fronts.

9 Stitch the appliqués to the background (refer to Fusible Web Appliqué, page 14). Stitch overlapping edges only once. If you wish, embroider around all appliqués (refer to Finishing Raw-Edge Appliqué with Embroidery, page 20).

Finishing

For more information about basting, marking, quilting, and binding your quilt, see Finishing the Quilt (page 23).

QUILTING

1 Layer the quilt top, batting, and backing; baste.

2 Quilt as desired.

WHAT I DID

I chose to quilt vertical straight lines within the building appliqués and radiating diagonal lines in the "street." I quilted the top of the quilt with wavy horizontal lines spaced to look like they were receding (see "Receding" Quilting, page 25).

BINDING

1 Trim the batting and backing flush with the quilt top.

2 Refer to Making Bias Binding (page 27) to make the binding, or use your favorite method.

3 Bind the quilt.

GRAND CANAL, 80″ × 60″, made by Casey York, quilted by Ann McNew, 2013

GRAND CANAL

FINISHED SIZE: 80″ × 60″

Perspective played a central role in European garden designs of the seventeenth and eighteenth centuries. At the royal palace of Versailles, André Le Nôtre used perspective to create the illusion of an endless vista, symbolizing the boundless reach of King Louis XIV's power. As part of his design, Le Nôtre added the mile-long Grand Canal to Versailles' east-west axis between 1668 and 1679. Inspired by his work, and among the more advanced projects in this book, this quilt draws upon and pays homage to the meaningful use of perspective by garden designers such as Le Nôtre.

43

materials

Unless otherwise noted, all measurements refer to 40˝-wide, 100% cotton quilting fabric. • The quilt shown features fabrics from Spoonflower.

WHITE PREMIUM MUSLIN: 2 yards 90˝ or wider for background, or 4½ yards for pieced background

BLUE: 1½ yards for canal

PINK: ¾ yard for parterres

MEDIUM GREEN: 1 yard for hedge tops

DARK GREEN: ¾ yard for right hedge side and topiaries

LIGHT GREEN: ¼ yard for left hedge side

GRAY-GREEN: ¼ yard for rear hedge sides and hedge ends

BACKING: 5 yards for pieced backing

BATTING: 68˝ × 88˝

BINDING: 1⅛ yards for bias binding

DOUBLE-SIDED, LIGHTWEIGHT FUSIBLE WEB, 15˝ WIDE: 6½ yards

EMBROIDERY FLOSS (optional):
3 skeins to match medium green; 2 skeins to match dark green; 1 skein each to match light green, gray-green, and blue

> **TIP** Like *Concrete Jungle*, this quilt features appliqués that are challenging because of their large size. Give yourself time and plenty of space for laying out your patterns and fabrics, and you'll find this quilt, while advanced, is not too difficult to tackle.

Assembling the Quilt Top

Refer to Appliqué Basics (pages 13–22) for details about printing the patterns and using the techniques needed for this project. The patterns have been changed from the original quilt to make them symmetrical for ease of construction. Larger patterns may require multiple widths of fusible web. *The appliqué patterns do not require any seam allowance. Use a ¼˝ seam allowance for piecing, unless otherwise stated.*

1 Prepare the *Grand Canal* appliqués (pages PDF3-1– PDF3-57). Refer to the materials list to determine the appliqué shapes to cut from each fabric. To reduce bulk, cut out the center of the fusible web from the large patterns before fusing to the wrong side of the appliqué fabric. **Note:** The dashed lines on the hedge and parterre appliqué patterns indicate places where the appliqué will be covered by an overlapping piece; trace and cut on the solid outer line.

2 Cut or piece background fabric to measure 80˝ × 60˝.

3 Find the center of the background fabric by folding it in half horizontally and vertically; the center is the point where the 2 folds meet. While the fabric is folded in half lengthwise, press to create a crease; this will serve as the horizon line.

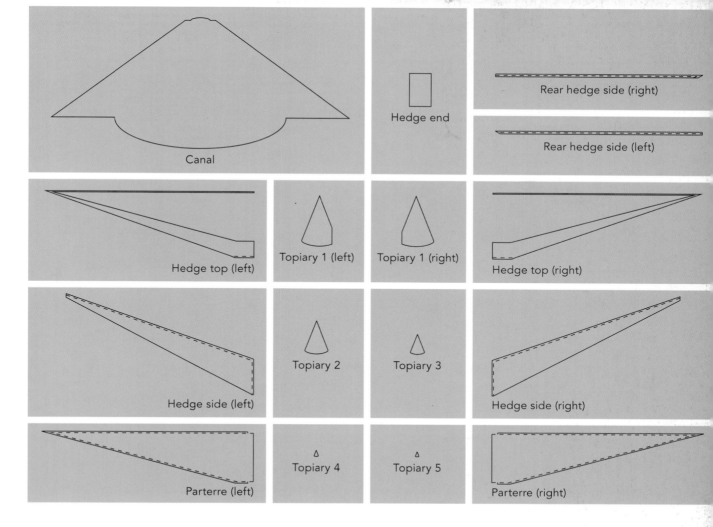

Canal

Hedge end

Rear hedge side (right)

Rear hedge side (left)

Hedge top (left)

Topiary 1 (left)

Topiary 1 (right)

Hedge top (right)

Hedge side (left)

Topiary 2

Topiary 3

Hedge side (right)

Parterre (left)

Topiary 4

Topiary 5

Parterre (right)

4 Following the placement diagrams, arrange the canal, hedge, and parterre appliqués on the background fabric in the following sequence, pinning well as you go:

a. First place the canal, centering it from left to right and aligning its top edge with the horizon line you pressed in Step 3.

b. Next, place the hedge tops, aligning their top edges with the horizon line and their outer edges with the edges of the background fabric. **FIGURE A**

c. Place the left and right hedge sides, then the parterres, tucking the edges beneath the edges of the hedge tops. Then place the rear hedge sides, tucking the edges under the hedge tops. **FIGURE B, PAGE 46**

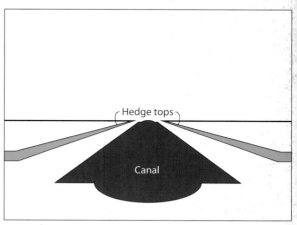

A Canal and hedge tops

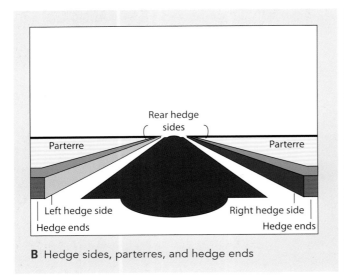

B Hedge sides, parterres, and hedge ends

C

d. Place the hedge ends so the top inner corners align with the intersections of the hedge tops and hedge sides. You may need to trim the outer edges along the edges of the background fabric. Tuck the edges of the hedge sides and tops beneath the hedge ends. **FIGURE B**

5 When you are satisfied with the placement, fuse the appliqués in place. Trim points or edges as needed for exact alignment (refer to Step 6, Assembling the Quilt Top, *Concrete Jungle*, page 40). **FIGURE C**

TIP Fusing the long, narrow hedge appliqués can be tricky. Start from the inside corners and work toward the edges. To ensure that the pieces overlap properly, fuse one appliqué at a time, beginning with the lowest layer and working toward the top.

6 Stitch the appliqués to the background (refer to Fusible Web Appliqué, page 14). Stitch overlapping edges only once.

7 Arrange the topiary appliqués, and pin. Fuse the topiaries in place and stitch around each. **FIGURE D**

8 If you wish, embroider around all appliqués (refer to Finishing Raw-Edge Appliqué with Embroidery, page 20).

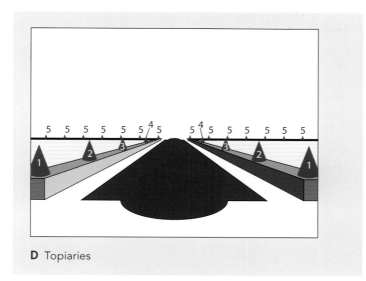

D Topiaries

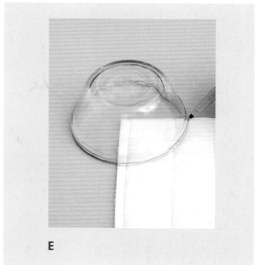

E

Finishing

For more information about basting, marking, quilting, and binding your quilt, see Finishing the Quilt (page 23).

QUILTING

1 Layer the quilt top, batting, and backing; baste.

2 Quilt as desired.

WHAT I DID

I chose to have the quilt quilted with a pattern of ripples in the canal, a dense floral pattern in the parterres, and pebbles in the two paths along the canal. The allover damask design in the top half of the quilt recalls Golden Age France. I chose to have the topiary appliqués outlined but left unquilted so they would appear to project from the quilt top, enhancing the three-dimensional effect.

BINDING

1 Trim the batting and backing flush with the quilt top.

2 To make inverse rounded corners, use a compass, a circle template, or a bowl or plate about 6″ in diameter as shown to trace a quarter-circle at each corner. Trim the quilt according to these markings. **FIGURE E**

3 Refer to Making Bias Binding (page 27) or use your favorite method to make the bias binding. Straight-grain binding will not work for the curved corners of this quilt.

4 Bind the quilt. You will need to miter each corner—there are 8 total—and ease the bias binding around the curves.

Euclid wrote the first treatise on optics about 300 BC, describing the convergence of parallel lines, the apparent height of the ground plane with distance, and the foreshortening of forms.

THE Natural

The Italian artist and architect Leon Battista Alberti was the first to codify a mathematical system for using linear perspective, which he published in his treatise *De pictura*, written and published in three parts over the years 1435–1436.

World

RIVER BEND, 35″ × 37″, made and quilted by Casey York, 2013

RIVER BEND

FINISHED SIZE: 35″ × 37″

This modern baby quilt was inspired by the dramatic thunderstorms that my family encounters while traveling around our home in the Midwest. Spurred by the deep blue ombré fabric, I attempted to capture the contrast of dark, heavy clouds against the streaming golden light that emerges after a storm. Simply constructed, the quilt consists of just two large appliqués on a pieced background.

materials

Unless otherwise noted, all measurements refer to 40˝-wide, 100% cotton quilting fabric.
• *This quilt features fabric from the V. and Co. Simply Color collection by Vanessa Christenson for Moda Fabrics.*

BLUE OMBRÉ: 1¼ yards* for sky

WHITE: ½ yard for river/ background

GREEN: ½ yard for river banks

BACKING: 1¼ yards (requires fabric at least 43˝ wide, or additional yardage to piece)

BATTING: 43˝ × 45˝

BINDING: ½ yard

LIGHTWEIGHT FUSIBLE WEB, 15˝ WIDE: 1¼ yards

EMBROIDERY FLOSS (*optional*): 1 skein to match fabric for grass

* *Only ¾ yard if using solid fabric*

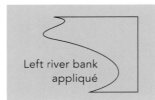

TIP If you cannot locate ombré fabric, this quilt top would also look lovely featuring a wide sky of solid pale blue or cloudy gray.

Assembling the Quilt Top

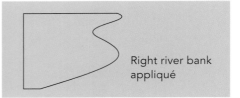

Left river bank appliqué

Right river bank appliqué

Refer to Appliqué Basics (pages 13–22) for details about printing the patterns and using the techniques needed for this project. Larger patterns may require multiple widths of fusible web. *The appliqué patterns do not require any seam allowance. Use a ¼˝ seam allowance for piecing, unless otherwise stated.*

1 Prepare the *River Bend* appliqués (page PDF4-1–PDF4-11). Refer to the materials list to determine the appliqué shapes to cut from each fabric. To reduce bulk, cut out the center of the fusible web from the large patterns before fusing to the wrong side of the green fabric.

2 Cut white fabric to measure 35˝ × 15¾˝.

3 Cut sky fabric to measure 35˝ × 21¾˝. If using ombré fabric, make sure the longer edge of the cut piece is parallel to the gradient of the ombré fabric. The dark-value edge will be the top of the sky, and the lighter value will be the bottom.

4 Sew the white piece to the bottom of the sky piece along the long edges to form a 35˝ × 37˝ background piece. **FIGURE A**

5 Arrange the appliqués on the background. Align the top edges of the 2 grass appliqués with the seam in the background and the sides of the white fabric; the 2 appliqués should almost touch at the center of the quilt. Pin in place. **FIGURE B**

6 When you are satisfied with the layout, fuse the appliqués down.

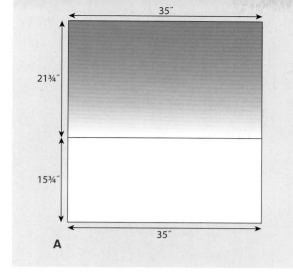

A

35"

21¾"

15¾"

35"

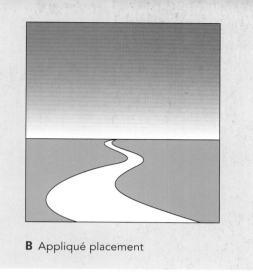

B Appliqué placement

TIP Begin fusing along the top and inner edges of the appliqués, smoothing them down with your iron as you work toward the outer and bottom edges.

7 Stitch the appliqués to the background (refer to Fusible Web Appliqué, page 14).

8 If you wish, embroider along the top and the inner wavy edges of the appliqués (refer to Finishing Raw-Edge Appliqué with Embroidery, page 20).

Finishing

For more information about basting, marking, quilting, and binding your quilt, see Finishing the Quilt (page 23).

QUILTING

1 Layer the quilt top, batting, and backing; baste.

2 Quilt as desired.

BINDING

1 Trim the batting and backing flush with the quilt top.

2 Refer to Making Bias Binding (page 27) to make the binding, or use your favorite method.

3 Bind the quilt.

WHAT I DID

I quilted the green areas with a series of wavy horizontal lines, which become farther apart toward the lower edge of the quilt (see "Receding" Quilting, page 25). I quilted the sky area in a cloud pattern and the river with a series of undulating lines suggesting the flow of water.

TIP I chose to use contrasting quilting thread colors to enhance the atmospheric look I was trying to achieve. I used a golden yellow for the grass areas and a silvery gray for the clouds and river.

CHICKEN SCRATCH, *60″ × 70″, made and quilted by Casey York, 2013*

CHICKEN SCRATCH

FINISHED SIZE: 60″ × 70″

Fabric choice plays a large role in the modern quilting movement, but I believe that modern quilts do not necessarily need to be made from modern-style fabrics. *Chicken Scratch* grew out of my desire to see whether I could make a modern quilt using 1930s reproduction–style fabrics. Many of these prints are based on the fabrics used to make chicken feed sacks during the 1930s; during the Great Depression, these sacks were repurposed for clothing. This quilt is a nod both to the resourcefulness of those who lived through this period and to contemporary DIY interests in upcycling, repurposing, and, yes, even raising chickens.

materials

Unless otherwise noted, all measurements refer to 40˝-wide, 100% cotton quilting fabric.

WHITE PREMIUM MUSLIN: 2 yards 90˝ or wider for background, or 4 yards for pieced background

LARGE-SCALE PRINT: ½ yard for Chicken 1

MEDIUM-LARGE-SCALE PRINT: ½ yard for Chicken 2

MEDIUM-SCALE PRINT: ⅜ yard or 1 fat quarter for Chicken 3

MEDIUM-SMALL-SCALE PRINT: ¼ yard or 1 fat eighth for Chicken 4

SMALL-SCALE PRINT: ⅛ yard or 1 fat eighth for Chicken 5

BACKING: 4½ yards for pieced backing

BATTING: 68˝ × 78˝

BINDING: 1 yard for bias binding

LIGHTWEIGHT FUSIBLE WEB, 15˝ WIDE: 2 yards

EMBROIDERY FLOSS (*optional*): 2 skeins to match appliqué fabric for Chicken 1; 1 skein each to match fabrics for Chickens 2, 3, 4, and 5

Assembling the Quilt Top

Refer to Appliqué Basics (pages 13–22) for details about printing the patterns and using the techniques needed for this project. Larger patterns may require multiple widths of fusible web. *The appliqué patterns do not require any seam allowance. Use a ¼˝ seam allowance for piecing, unless otherwise stated.*

1 Prepare the *Chicken Scratch* appliqués (page PDF5-1– PDF5-12). Refer to the materials list to determine the appliqué shapes to cut from each fabric. If you wish, cut out the center of the fusible web from the largest patterns (Chickens 1 and 2) before fusing to the wrong side of the fabric.

2 Cut or piece background fabric to measure 60˝ × 70˝.

3 Fold the background fabric in half widthwise and press to create a crease. This crease will serve as the horizon.

4 Starting at the horizon, mark a series of horizontal lines moving toward the lower edge of the background fabric as follows: Mark the first line ¼˝ from the horizon, and then add ¼˝ to each subsequent measurement. The second line will be ½˝ from the first, the third ¾˝ from the second, and so on. This method is identical to that described in "Receding" Quilting (page 25), except that the measurements are based on ¼˝ instead of ½˝. These lines will guide your placement of the appliqués and serve as your quilting lines.

Chicken 1 appliqué

Chicken 2 appliqué

Chicken 3 appliqué

Chicken 4 appliqué

Chicken 5 appliqué

5 Following the placement and quilting diagram (at right) and using the horizontal markings for reference, arrange the appliqués on the background fabric. When you are satisfied with their placement, use an iron to fuse them permanently into place according to the manufacturer's directions.

TIP When placing the chicken appliqués, it helps to note that each chicken has at least one foot on the "ground." This foot should lie parallel to the horizontal lines you marked in Step 4.

6 Stitch the appliqués to the background to secure (refer to Fusible Web Appliqué, page 14).

7 If you wish, embroider around all appliqués (refer to Finishing Raw-Edge Appliqué with Embroidery, page 20).

Placement and quilting diagram

CHICKEN
SCRATCH

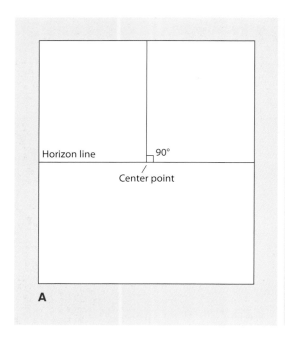

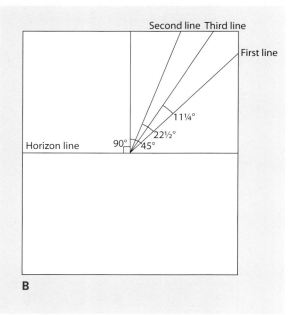

Finishing

For more information about basting, marking, quilting, and binding your quilt, see Finishing the Quilt (page 23).

QUILTING

1 Layer the quilt top, batting, and backing; baste.

2 If necessary, re-mark the horizontal lines that you drew in Assembling the Quilt Top, Step 4 (page 56).

3 Fold the quilt top in half vertically and mark the center point of the horizon line. Using a long ruler, mark a vertical line from this center point to the center of the top edge of the quilt. Mark additional lines radiating from this center point of the horizon to the top and side edges of the quilt. I find it easiest to mark radiating lines by estimating the halfway point between 2 adjacent lines. **FIGURES A & B**

4 Using a walking foot, quilt along the marked lines.

C

BINDING

1 Trim the batting and backing flush with the quilt top.

2 To make rounded corners, place a compass, a circle template, or a bowl or plate about 10″ in diameter adjacent to the quilt edges at each corner. Trace along its outer edge. Trim the quilt according to these markings. **FIGURE C**

3 Refer to Making Bias Binding (page 27) or use your favorite method to make the bias binding. Straight-grain binding will not work for the curved corners of this quilt.

4 Bind the quilt.

UPWARD, 50˝ × 40˝, made and quilted by Casey York, 2013

UPWARD

FINISHED SIZE: 50″ × 40″

Perspective governs how we perceive not only our surroundings but also the sky above us, as illustrated by the shrinking kites and gulls in this quilt. For some reason, I always associate kite flying with windy Canal Park in my hometown of Duluth, Minnesota. The park naturally is also home to flocks of seagulls. Since I conceived of this quilt as a companion to *Onwards* (page 7), I was delighted to learn that the designer of the fabric featured in *Onwards*, Violet Craft, had designed a new fabric collection named Waterfront Park that complemented this quilt concept perfectly. It even featured an aerial lift bridge similar to Duluth's in one of the prints, which I used for the back of *Upward*. To me, the fabric evokes the wide skies and sparkling waters of the lakeshore. I tried to capture the same impression of boundless space in the quilt design itself.

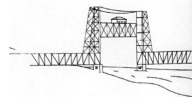

Bridgetown from the Waterfront Park collection by Violet Craft for Michael Miller Fabrics

Photo by Casey York

Aerial lift bridge, Canal Park, Duluth, Minnesota

61

materials

Unless otherwise noted, all measurements refer to 40˝-wide, 100% cotton quilting fabric.

• *The quilt shown features the Waterfront Park collection by Violet Craft for Michael Miller Fabrics.*

WHITE BACKGROUND: 1½ yards

CORAL: ⅓ yard for Kites 1 and 4

YELLOW: ¼ yard or 1 fat eighth for Kite 2

BLUE: ¼ yard or 1 fat eighth for Kite 3

GRAY: ⅜ yard for seagulls

BACKING: 2⅞ yards

BATTING: 48˝ × 58˝

BINDING: ½ yard for straight-grain binding or ⅞ yard for bias binding

LIGHTWEIGHT FUSIBLE WEB, 15˝ WIDE: 1 yard

EMBROIDERY FLOSS: 1 skein each of coral, yellow, and blue for kite tails; 1 skein gray perle cotton, size 5 or 8, for kite strings; *optional:* 1 more skein coral and 1 skein gray for embroidery around appliqués

Assembling the Quilt Top

Refer to Appliqué Basics (pages 13–22) for details about printing the patterns and using the techniques needed for this project. *The appliqué patterns do not require any seam allowance. Use a ¼˝ seam allowance for piecing, unless otherwise stated.*

1 Prepare the *Upward* appliqués (page PDF6-1–PDF6-7). Refer to the materials list to determine the appliqué shapes to cut from each fabric.

2 Cut or piece the background fabric to measure 50˝ × 40˝.

3 Find the center of the background fabric by folding it in half horizontally and vertically; the center is the point where the 2 folds meet.

4 Following the placement diagram, arrange the appliqués on the background fabric.

5 When you are satisfied with the layout, fuse the appliqués in place.

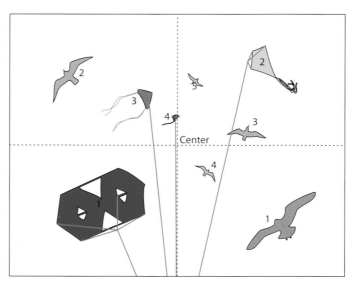

Placement diagram

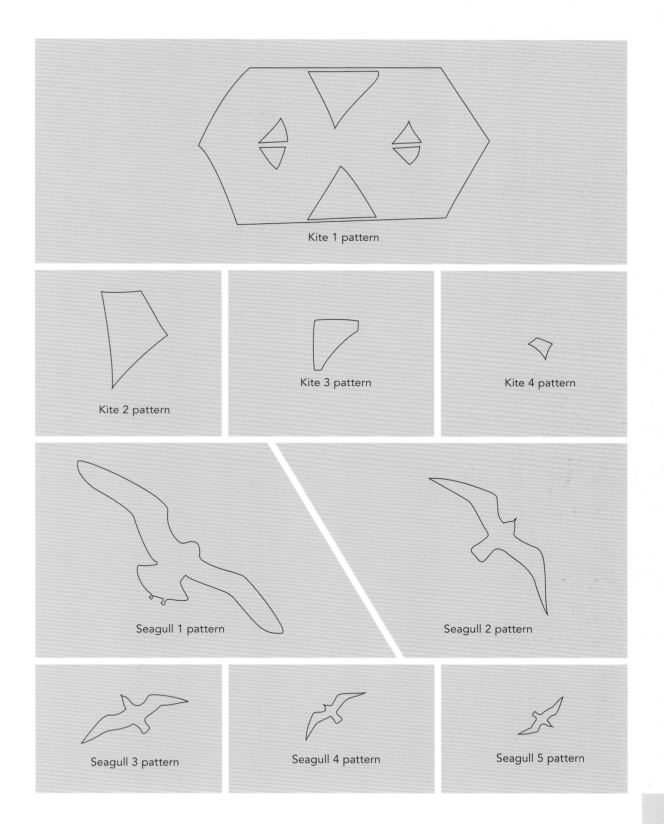

Kite 1 pattern

Kite 2 pattern

Kite 3 pattern

Kite 4 pattern

Seagull 1 pattern

Seagull 2 pattern

Seagull 3 pattern

Seagull 4 pattern

Seagull 5 pattern

6 Stitch the appliqués to the background (refer to Fusible Web Appliqué, page 14).

7 If you wish, embroider around all appliqués (refer to Finishing Raw-Edge Appliqué with Embroidery, page 20).

8 Referring to the placement diagram (page 62), use a removable marker to trace the kite tail patterns (page PDF6-1) onto each kite.

TIP If you are using a pale background fabric, you can simply place the kite tail patterns beneath the fabric and trace.

9 Embroider the kite tails using a backstitch (page 22).

TIP I used fewer strands of embroidery floss for the tails of the smallest kites to increase the illusion that they were farther away. I used 3 strands of floss for Kites 1 and 2, 2 strands for Kite 3, and 1 strand for Kite 4.

10 Following the placement diagram, use a ruler to mark a straight line from each kite to the lower edge of the quilt top to represent the kite strings. Connect the top point of each kite string to the corners of the corresponding kite as indicated in the placement diagram.

11 Embroider the kite strings using gray perle cotton and a stem stitch (pages 22).

Finishing

For more information about basting, marking, quilting, and binding your quilt, see Finishing the Quilt (page 23).

QUILTING

1 Layer the quilt top, batting, and backing; baste.

2 Starting 7″ above the center point of the background, draw a small circle 2″ in diameter using the pattern (page PDF6-1). Starting on the left-hand side of the circle, draw a freehand spiral counterclockwise around the center circle, roughly 1½″ away from the center circle. With each pass around, increase the distance between the spirals by approximately another ¼″. Continue marking until you reach the edges of the background fabric.

TIP Do not quilt over the appliquéd forms; leaving the appliqués unquilted will create the illusion that the continuous quilted spiral is behind them.

3 Using a walking foot, quilt along the marked lines.

BINDING

1 Trim the batting and backing flush with the quilt top.

2 Refer to Making Bias Binding (page 27) or use your favorite method to make the binding.

3 Bind the quilt.

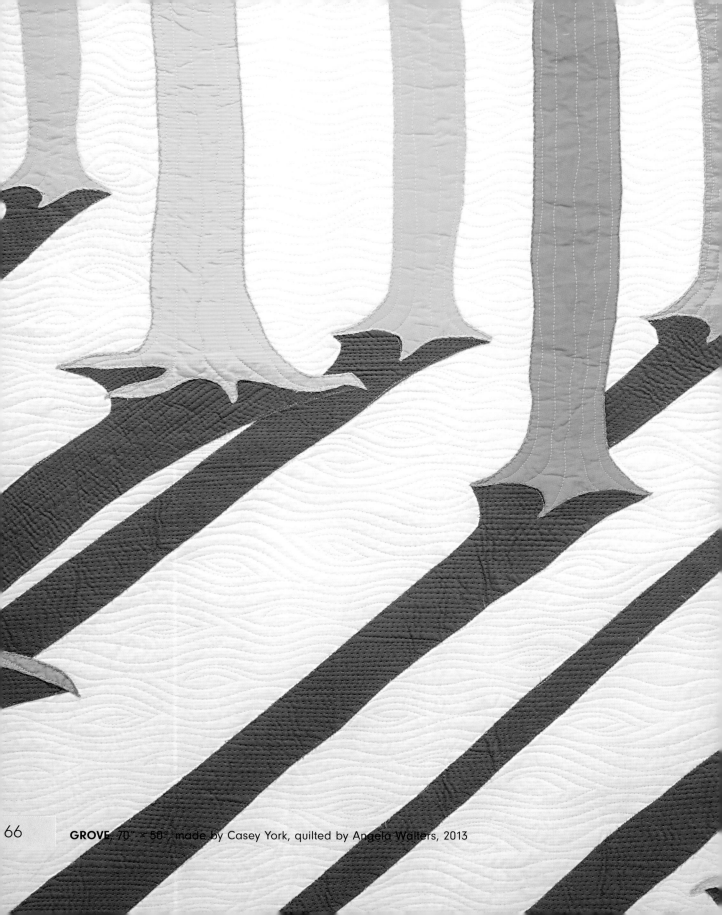

GROVE, 70" × 50", made by Casey York, quilted by Angela Walters, 2013

GROVE

FINISHED SIZE: 70″ × 50″

This quilt evokes the dramatic light and shadows produced by the late afternoon sun filtering through a stand of trees. Bright, sour greens and yellows marry with elongated shadows to create a dynamic interplay of light and color.

materials

Unless otherwise noted, all measurements refer to 40˝-wide, 100% cotton quilting fabric.

WHITE PREMIUM MUSLIN:
2 yards 90˝ or wider for background, or 4 yards for pieced background

GRAY: 1½ yards for shadows

LIGHT YELLOW: ¾ yard for Trees 1 and 7

DEEP YELLOW: ½ yard for Trees 4 and 10

YELLOW-GREEN: 1½ yards for Trees 3, 6, and 8

APPLE GREEN: ½ yard for Trees 5 and 11

OLIVE GREEN: ½ yard for Trees 2 and 9

BACKING: 4½ yards for pieced backing

BATTING: 58˝ × 78˝

BINDING: ¾ yard for straight-grain binding or 1 yard for bias binding

LIGHTWEIGHT FUSIBLE WEB, 15˝ WIDE: 7 yards

EMBROIDERY FLOSS (optional):
8 skeins to match shadow appliqué fabric, 2 skeins to match each tree appliqué fabric

Assembling the Quilt Top

Refer to Appliqué Basics (pages 13–22) for details about printing the patterns and using the techniques needed for this project. Larger patterns may require multiple widths of fusible web. *The appliqué patterns do not require any seam allowance. Use a ¼˝ seam allowance for piecing, unless otherwise stated.*

1 Prepare the *Grove* appliqués (page PDF7-1–PDF7-64). Refer to the materials list and the instructions on the patterns to determine the appliqué shapes to cut from each fabric. *Note that the same pattern may be used for multiple trees or different fabrics.* Transfer the numbers from the patterns to the fusible web tracings. The trees are numbered from right to left across the quilt, and the tree shadow appliqués are numbered to match the trees to which they correspond (Tree Shadow 1 goes with Tree 1, for example), *not* the order in which they are placed across the quilt top. There is 1 shadow that corresponds to an unseen tree.

TIP To give the trees a more organic appearance, I followed the pattern lines less closely than usual when tracing the appliqués.

2 Cut or piece background fabric to measure 70˝ × 50˝.

3 Referring to the placement diagram (page 70), work from right to left to arrange the tree appliqués in order of their numbers. Align the top edge of each tree appliqué with the top edge of the background fabric. Pin in place.

4 Arrange the corresponding shadow appliqué for each tree, aligning the straight lower edges of the appliqués with the bottom edge of the background fabric. Tuck the top of each shadow beneath the roots of its tree, making sure that the roots completely cover the tops of the shadows. Trim the shadow appliqués if necessary to make them fit under the tree roots. Pin in place.

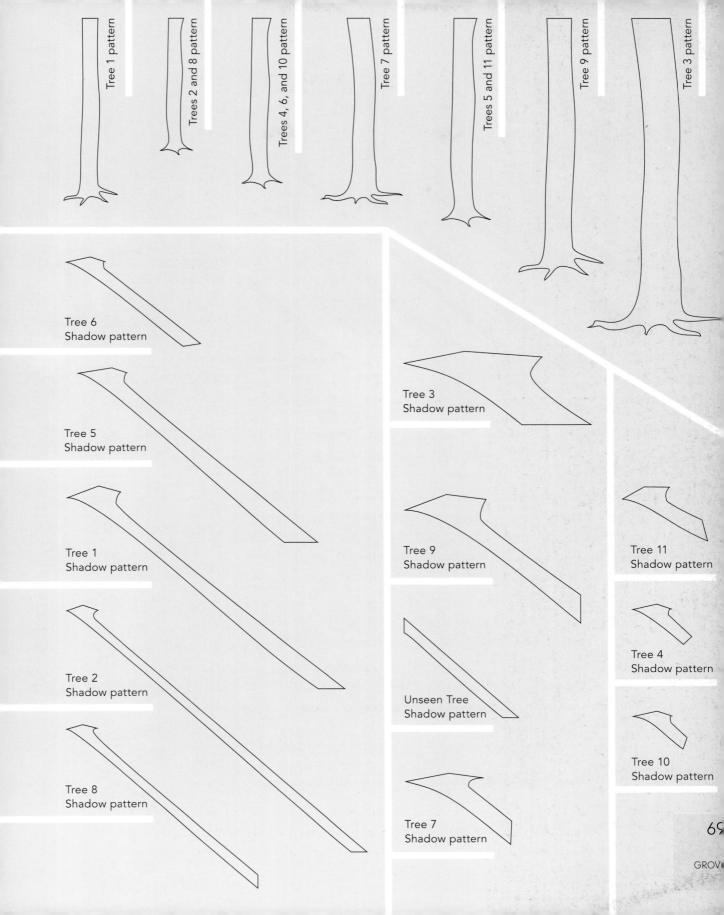

Tree 1 pattern

Trees 2 and 8 pattern

Trees 4, 6, and 10 pattern

Tree 7 pattern

Trees 5 and 11 pattern

Tree 9 pattern

Tree 3 pattern

Tree 6
Shadow pattern

Tree 5
Shadow pattern

Tree 1
Shadow pattern

Tree 2
Shadow pattern

Tree 8
Shadow pattern

Tree 3
Shadow pattern

Tree 9
Shadow pattern

Unseen Tree
Shadow pattern

Tree 7
Shadow pattern

Tree 11
Shadow pattern

Tree 4
Shadow pattern

Tree 10
Shadow pattern

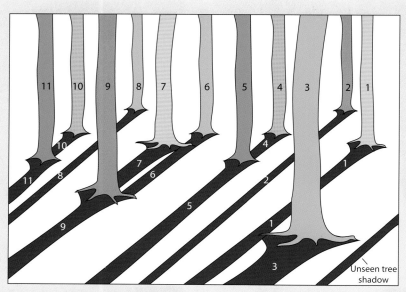

A Placement diagram

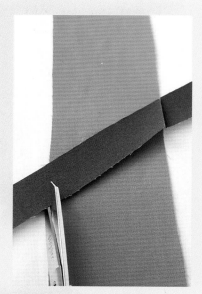

B Trim overlapping shadows just inside edges of trees.

5 Place the unseen tree shadow appliqué at the bottom right corner of the quilt top, following the placement diagram as a guide. **FIGURE A**

6 At this point, you will notice that Tree Shadows 1, 2, and 8 cross over the trees adjacent to them. Carefully cut these shadow appliqués where they intersect a tree, trimming each end of the shadow just inside the sides of the tree. Tuck the trimmed ends beneath the tree appliqués, aligning them to appear to form a continuous line. **FIGURE B**

7 Tuck the ends of the truncated shadow appliqués (Tree Shadows 4, 6, 7, and 10) beneath the adjacent tree appliqués, trimming if necessary.

TIP Trimming the appliqués as they are placed and pinned to the background, instead of when they are first cut from the web, ensures that edges will match perfectly.

8 When you are satisfied with the layout, fuse the appliqués in place.

9 Stitch the appliqués to the background (refer to Fusible Web Appliqué, page 14).

10 If you wish, embroider around the tree shapes and shadows (refer to Finishing Raw-Edge Appliqué with Embroidery, page 20).

TIP For this quilt, I chose to embroider around the tree appliqués but not around the shadows. The small amount of fraying that will occur to the shadow fabrics will contribute to the effect of shadows projected onto grassy ground, enhancing the appearance of the quilt.

Finishing

For more information about basting, marking, quilting, and binding your quilt, see Finishing the Quilt (page 23).

QUILTING

1 Layer the quilt top, batting, and backing; baste.

2 Quilt as desired.

WHAT I DID

I had my *Grove* quilted following the contours of the appliqués; however, this quilt also would be lovely quilted with an allover pattern. I had the background areas quilted with a wood-grain pattern. Vertical lines that get closer together as they approach the edges of the tree appliqués enhance the illusion of round tree trunks.

BINDING

1 Trim the batting and backing flush with the quilt top.

2 Refer to Making Bias Binding (page 27) or use your favorite method to make the binding.

3 Bind the quilt.

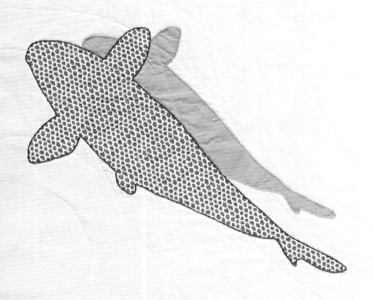

72 **RIPPLES**, 54″ × 72″, made and quilted by Casey York, 2013

RIPPLES

FINISHED SIZE: 54″ × 72″

Most of the quilts in this book use some form of perspective to create the illusion of depth and distance, but simple shadows also can be effective. In this quilt, graceful koi silhouettes overlap with slightly smaller shadows to give a sense of movement and depth. I chose to quilt this project with simple concentric circles that overlap the koi and each other, suggesting ripples on the surface of a pond.

materials

Unless otherwise noted, all measurements refer to 40˝-wide, 100% cotton quilting fabric.

WHITE PREMIUM MUSLIN: 1⅝ yards 90˝ or wider for background, or 4⅛ yards for pieced background

ORANGES: ⅓ yard each of 3 different orange prints for Koi 1, 3, and 4; and ⅜ yard each of 2 different orange prints for Koi 2 and 5

GRAY: ¾ yard for shadows

BACKING: 4⅝ yards for pieced backing

BATTING: 62˝ × 80˝

BINDING: ⅔ yard for straight-grain binding or 1 yard for bias binding

LIGHTWEIGHT FUSIBLE WEB, 15˝ WIDE: 3⅓ yards

EMBROIDERY FLOSS (*optional*): 1 skein to match each appliqué fabric

Assembling the Quilt Top

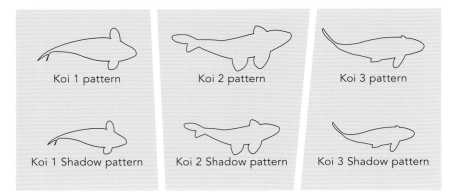

Koi 1 pattern   Koi 2 pattern   Koi 3 pattern

Koi 1 Shadow pattern   Koi 2 Shadow pattern   Koi 3 Shadow pattern

Refer to Appliqué Basics (pages 13–22) for details about printing the patterns and using the techniques needed for this project. *The appliqué patterns do not require any seam allowance. Use a ¼˝ seam allowance for piecing, unless otherwise stated.*

1 Prepare the *Ripples* appliqués (page PDF8-1–PDF8-29). Refer to the materials list to determine the appliqué shapes to cut from each fabric.

2 Cut or piece background fabric to measure 54˝ × 72˝.

3 Find the center of the background fabric by folding it in half horizontally and vertically; the center is the point where the 2 folds meet.

4 Beginning with the central Koi 1 and its shadow, position each koi and shadow pair on the background according to the placement diagram. Koi and their shadows will overlap. Position all appliqués at least 2˝ from the outer edges of the background.

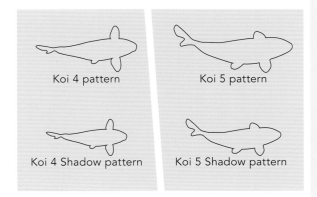

Koi 4 pattern

Koi 5 pattern

Koi 4 Shadow pattern

Koi 5 Shadow pattern

A Placement and quilting diagram

TIP Pay special attention to how you space the koi and their shadows. Space all the shadow pieces the same distance from the corresponding koi pieces to create the illusion that the fish are floating above solid ground. Use the distance from the tips of the koi silhouettes to the head and tail tips of the shadows to gauge the spacing. Once you are satisfied with the spacing of the shadows, pin them to their matching koi appliqués so you can adjust the pairs without disturbing the relative position of koi and shadow to one another.

5 When you are satisfied with the placement, fuse the appliqués in place. **FIGURE A**

6 Stitch the appliqués to the background (refer to Fusible Web Appliqué, page 14).

7 If you wish, embroider around all appliqués (refer to Finishing Raw-Edge Appliqué with Embroidery, page 17).

Finishing

For more information about basting, marking, quilting, and binding your quilt, see Finishing the Quilt (page 23).

QUILTING

1 Layer the quilt top, batting, and backing; baste.

2 Print the circle pattern (page PDF8-1) and use it to mark a circle on the quilt top. Mark around the circle, 2″ from the edge, and use these marks to draw a concentric circle. Mark 2″ from the edges of the second circle and use the marks to draw a third circle. Repeat until the "ripples" are as large as you want them—I like about 9–13 concentric circles for each set of ripples. **FIGURE B**

Repeat this process across the quilt until the top has enough marks to be quilted with fairly even density. To create the appearance of randomly occurring ripples, I did not center ripples on the koi but rather placed them independently. For the most natural effect, avoid aligning the initial circles horizontally or vertically.

Refer to the placement and quilting diagram (page 75) if you would like a guide.

> **TIP** Unlike most of the quilts in this book, *Ripples* uses quilting lines that cross over the appliqués. This creates the illusion that the koi are floating on a different plane than the ripples above them.

3 Using a walking foot, quilt along the marked lines.

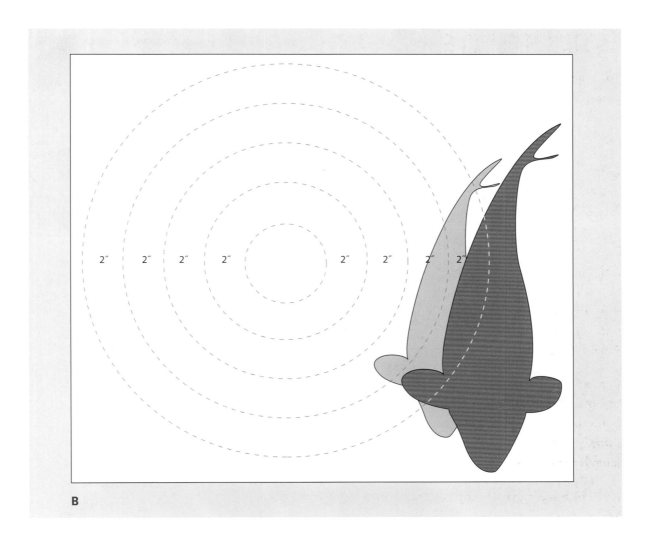

B

BINDING

1 Trim the batting and backing flush with the quilt top.

2 Refer to Making Bias Binding (page 27) or use your favorite method to make the binding.

3 Bind the quilt.

KEEP THING
PERSPECT

Other ways of representing depth on a two-dimensional surface include overlapping forms and decreasing their clarity and the intensity of their color with apparent distance, which is sometimes known as *aerial perspective*.

Concepts

BABY BLOCKS, 50″ × 52″, made and quilted by Casey York, 2013

BABY BLOCKS

FINISHED SIZE: 50″ × 52″

Cubes are among the most recognizable three-dimensional forms. This quilt takes advantage of this fact to create the illusion of stacked baby blocks. Perfectly sized for a baby or child, this quilt is quick to assemble but creates a big impression.

Unless otherwise noted, all measurements refer to 40″-wide, 100% cotton quilting fabric.

LIGHT GRAY: 1½ yards for upper background

DARK GRAY: 1½ yards for lower background

WHITE: 1 yard for blocks

YELLOW, TURQUOISE, AND ORANGE: ½ yard each for block border and letter

BACKING: 3⅜ yards for pieced backing

BATTING: 58″ × 60″

BINDING: 1 yard for bias binding

LIGHTWEIGHT FUSIBLE WEB, 15″ WIDE: 2½ yards

EMBROIDERY FLOSS (*optional*): 1 skein to match each block

Assembling the Quilt Top

Refer to Appliqué Basics (pages 13–22) for details about printing the patterns and using the techniques needed for this project. Larger patterns may require multiple widths of fusible web. *The appliqué patterns do not require any seam allowance. Use a ¼″ seam allowance for piecing, unless otherwise stated.*

1 Prepare the *Baby Blocks* appliqués (page PDF9-1–PDF9-27). Refer to the materials list to determine the appliqué shapes to cut from each fabric. **Note:** The dashed lines on the B and C Block Body appliqué patterns indicate places where the appliqué will be covered by an overlapping piece; trace and cut on the solid outer line.

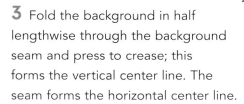 To ensure that the colored border of each block completely covers the white background, cut out the block border appliqués just *outside* the traced line.

2 Cut light gray and dark gray fabrics to measure 50″ × 26¼″ each. Sew, right sides together, along the long edge to form a 50″ × 52″ rectangle for the background. Press the seam open.

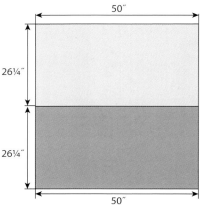

3 Fold the background in half lengthwise through the background seam and press to crease; this forms the vertical center line. The seam forms the horizontal center line.

4 Following the placement diagram (page 84), arrange the white block body appliqués on the background fabric. Pin in place. Check to make sure that the colored block border appliqués align with the white block body appliqués, but do not pin yet. **FIGURE A**

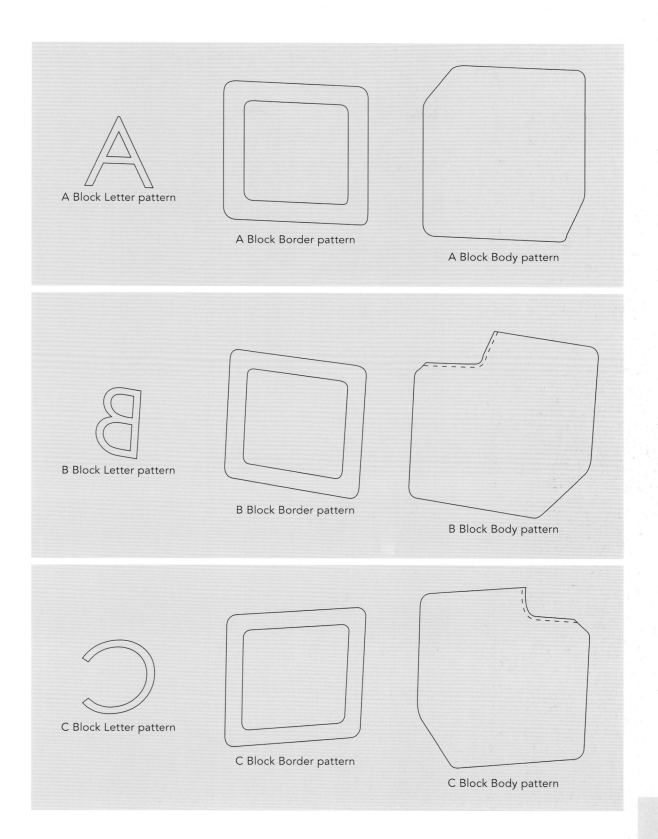

A Block Letter pattern

A Block Border pattern

A Block Body pattern

B Block Letter pattern

B Block Border pattern

B Block Body pattern

C Block Letter pattern

C Block Border pattern

C Block Body pattern

A Placement diagram

5 When you are satisfied with the placement, fuse the white block body appliqués in place.

6 Arrange the colored block border and letter appliqués on top of the white block bodies. **FIGURE A**

7 When you are satisfied with the placement, fuse the colored appliqués in place.

8 Stitch the appliqués to the background to secure (refer to Fusible Web Appliqué, page 14).

9 If you wish, embroider around each appliqué (refer to Finishing Raw-Edge Appliqué with Embroidery, page 20).

B

Finishing

For more information about basting, marking, quilting, and binding your quilt, see Finishing the Quilt (page 23).

QUILTING

1 Layer the quilt top, batting, and backing; baste.

2 Quilt as desired.

WHAT I DID

I quilted the top half of the background with a repeating cursive alphabet and the lower half of the background with evenly spaced horizontal lines. I quilted around each block border and letter, and used angled lines matching the block faces to quilt the white portion of each block.

BINDING

1 Trim the batting and backing flush with the quilt top.

2 To make rounded corners, place a compass, a circle template, or a bowl or plate with a 6″ diameter adjacent to the quilt edges at each corner. Trace along its outer edge. Trim the quilt according to these markings. **FIGURE B**

3 Refer to Making Bias Binding (page 27) or use your favorite method to make the bias binding. Straight-grain binding will not work for the curved corners of this quilt.

4 Bind the quilt.

STILL LIFE, 24˝ × 18˝, made and quilted by Casey York, 2013

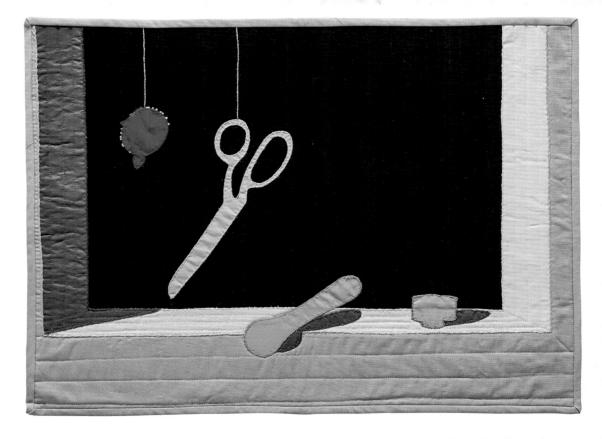

STILL LIFE
(Homage to Juan Sánchez Cotán)

FINISHED SIZE: 24″ × 18″

The seventeenth-century Spanish painter Juan Sánchez Cotán is known for his enigmatic still-life paintings, which feature humble vegetables and game isolated in austere settings. His practice of placing starkly lit objects before a dark background caught on quickly with his fellow artists, becoming typical of Spanish still-life paintings. Yet Sánchez Cotán's compositions retain a strikingly modern appearance. This small wall quilt draws directly from the artist's work *Quince, Cabbage, Melon, and Cucumber.*

Juan Sánchez Cotán; **QUINCE, CABBAGE, MELON, AND CUCUMBER**; oil on canvas, 27⅛″ × 33¼″, ca. 1602; gift of Anne R. and Amy Putnam, The San Diego Museum of Art, 1945.43

materials

Unless otherwise noted, all measurements refer to 40˝-wide, 100% cotton quilting fabric.

BLACK: ⅝ yard for background

MEDIUM GRAY: ⅝ yard for wall

LIGHT GRAY: ½ yard for ledge

DARK GRAY: ¼ yard or 1 fat quarter for shadows

RED: ⅛ yard or 1 fat eighth, or 3˝ × 3˝ scrap, for pincushion

SILVER GRAY: ⅛ or 1 fat eighth for scissors

ORANGE: ⅛ yard or 1 fat eighth for rotary cutter

GREEN: ⅛ yard or 1 fat eighth for spools of thread

BACKING: ⅝ yard

BATTING: 22˝ × 28˝

BINDING: ⅓ yard for straight-grain binding or ⅝ yard for bias binding

LIGHTWEIGHT FUSIBLE WEB, 15˝ WIDE: 1¾ yards

EMBROIDERY FLOSS: 1 skein light gray for hanging scissors and pincushion, 1 skein white perle cotton for pinheads on pincushion; *optional:* 1 skein each to match remaining appliqué fabrics for embroidery around appliqués

Assembling the Quilt Top

Refer to Appliqué Basics (pages 13–22) for details about printing the patterns and using the techniques needed for this project. Larger patterns may require multiple widths of fusible web. *The appliqué patterns do not require any seam allowance. Use a ¼˝ seam allowance for piecing, unless otherwise stated.*

1 Prepare the *Still Life* appliqués (page PDF10-1–PDF10-14). Refer to the materials list to determine the appliqué shapes to cut from each fabric. **Note:** The dashed lines on some of the appliqué patterns indicate places where the appliqué will be covered by an overlapping piece. Trace and cut on the solid outer line.

2 Cut background fabric to measure 24˝ × 18˝. Find the center of the background fabric by folding it in half horizontally and vertically; the center is the point where the 2 folds meet.

3 Position the wall appliqué on the background, aligning the outer edges of the appliqué with the sides and bottom edge of the background fabric.

4 Referring to the placement diagram (page 90), place the ledge and ledge shadow appliqués. Tuck the edges of the ledge appliqué under the edges of the shadow and wall appliqués. Tuck the left edge of the ledge shadow appliqué beneath the edge of the wall appliqué. Pin in place.

TIP Use the center point on the placement diagram and the center point you marked on the background fabric to place the sewing implement appliqués.

5 Referring to the placement diagram (page 90), arrange the remaining appliqués on the background; pin in place. Add the shadows beneath the rotary cutter and spools of thread, tucking them just underneath each corresponding shape.

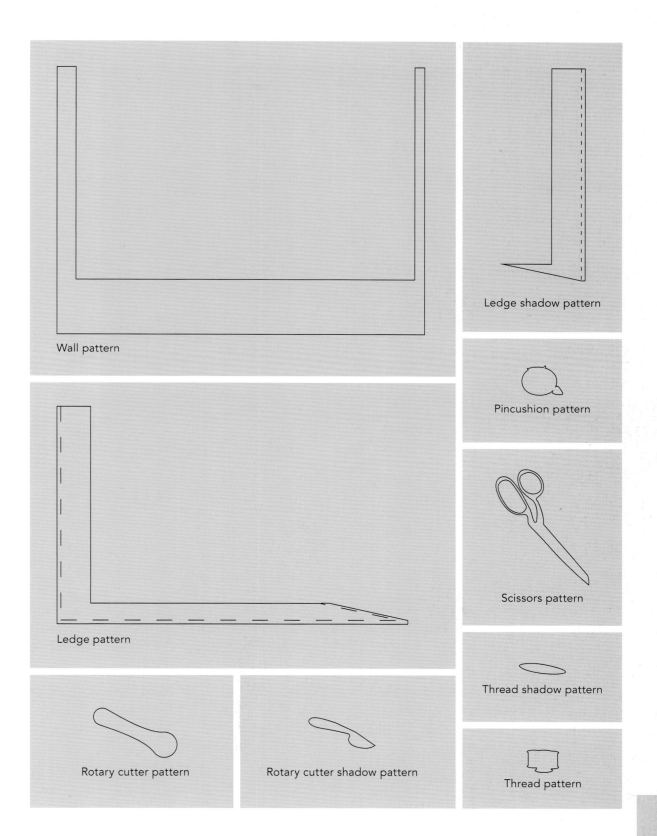

Wall pattern

Ledge shadow pattern

Ledge pattern

Pincushion pattern

Scissors pattern

Rotary cutter pattern

Rotary cutter shadow pattern

Thread shadow pattern

Thread pattern

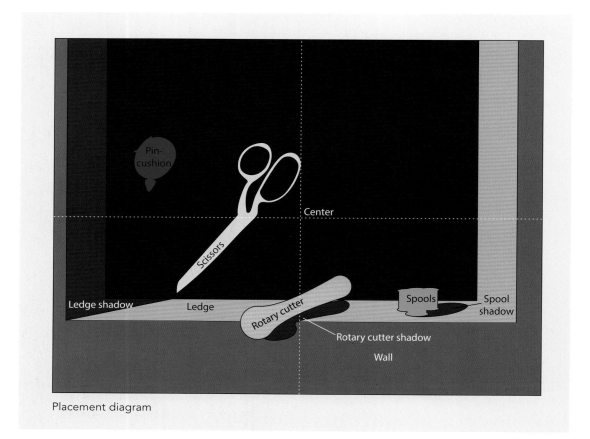

Placement diagram

6 When you are satisfied with the placement, fuse the appliqués in place.

7 Stitch the appliqués to the background (refer to Fusible Web Appliqué, page 14).

8 If you wish, embroider around all appliqués (refer to Finishing Raw-Edge Appliqué with Embroidery, page 20).

9 Mark a vertical line from the tops of the pincushion and scissors to the top edge of the background fabric. Using 2 strands of light gray embroidery floss, embroider along the marked lines with a stem stitch or backstitch (page 22). Using white perle cotton, make a series of French knots (page 22) along the upper perimeter of the pincushion to represent pinheads.

Finishing

For more information about basting, marking, quilting, and binding your quilt, see Finishing the Quilt (page 23).

QUILTING

1 Layer the quilt top, batting, and backing; baste.

2 Quilt as desired.

WHAT I DID

I quilted the background, wall, and ledge with closely spaced parallel lines and left the rest of the appliqués unquilted to enhance their three-dimensional appearance.

BINDING

1 Trim the batting and backing flush with the quilt top.

2 Refer to Making Bias Binding (page 27) or use your favorite method to make the binding.

3 Bind the quilt.

FLIGHT PLAN, 48″ × 59″, made and quilted by Casey York, 2013

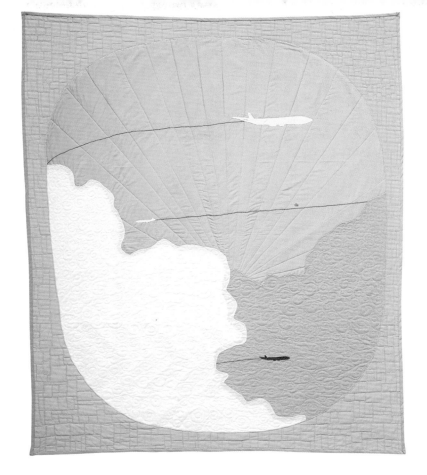

FLIGHT PLAN

FINISHED SIZE: 48″ × 59″

Growing up as the daughter of a pilot, I spent a lot of time in airplanes. One of my favorite parts of flying remains seeing the tiny silhouettes of other planes—they seem close by, but their size betrays their distance. I also love the difference in scale between airliners—which seem so huge on the ground—and the clouds that dwarf them as they climb.

materials

Unless otherwise noted, all measurements refer to 40˝-wide, 100% cotton quilting fabric.

BEIGE: 3½ yards for window

LIGHT BLUE: 2⅛ yards for sky

WHITE: 1½ yards for white cloud and Planes 1 and 2

LIGHT GRAY: 1 yard for gray cloud

DARK GRAY: 1 fat eighth or scrap at least 3˝ × 6˝ for Plane 3

BACKING: 3½ yards for pieced backing

BATTING: 56˝ × 67˝

BINDING: ⅝ yard for straight-grain binding or 1 yard for bias binding

LIGHTWEIGHT FUSIBLE WEB, 15˝ WIDE: 5 yards

EMBROIDERY FLOSS: 1 skein red; *optional:* 2 skeins to match window, 1 skein each to match white and gray clouds and Plane 3

Assembling the Quilt Top

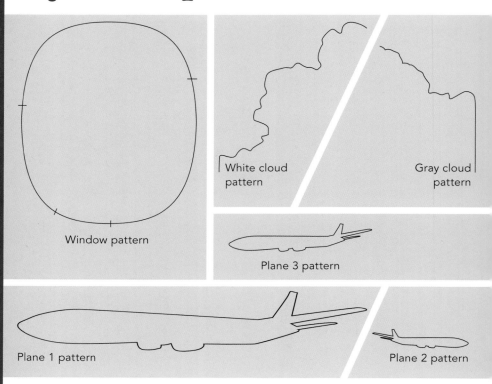

Window pattern

White cloud pattern

Gray cloud pattern

Plane 3 pattern

Plane 1 pattern

Plane 2 pattern

Refer to Appliqué Basics (pages 13–22) for details about printing the patterns and using the techniques needed for this project. Larger patterns may require multiple widths of fusible web. *The appliqué patterns do not require any seam allowance. Use a ¼˝ seam allowance for piecing, unless otherwise stated. Note: This project differs from the others in that it is reverse appliqué. Follow the steps in the order given for the easiest assembly.*

1 Print out and assemble the paper patterns (pages PDF11-1– PDF11-33) following the schematics on the patterns. Set aside.

2 Cut beige fabric into 2 pieces, each 59˝ long. Stitch, right sides together, along a long side. Press and trim evenly from each long side to measure 48˝ × 59˝. **FIGURE A**

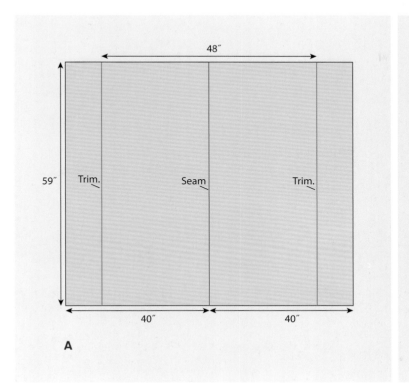

48″

59″

Trim.

Seam

Trim.

40″ 40″

A

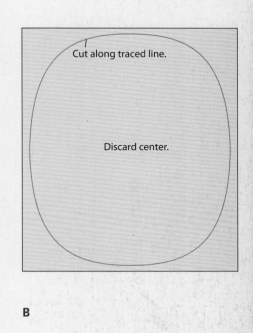

Cut along traced line.

Discard center.

B

3 Find the center of the resulting rectangle by folding it in half horizontally and vertically; the center is the point where the 2 folds meet.

4 Trace the window pattern (pages PDF11-15–PDF11-32) onto fusible web and cut out, leaving a ½″ margin on either side of the traced line. There are guide marks on the window pattern to help place the cloud appliqués later, but these do *not* need to be transferred to the fusible web.

TIP The large size of the window pattern and appliqués can make this quilt challenging. Because you will need to trace the window pattern onto the fusible web in multiple segments, it is helpful to number each segment. When fusing the pattern to the fabric, take care to line up the traced markings.

5 Center the fusible window outline on the *wrong* side of the pieced beige rectangle and fuse it in place. Cut away *inside* the fused window oval along the traced line and discard the center. **FIGURE B**

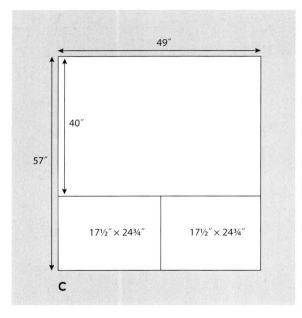

C

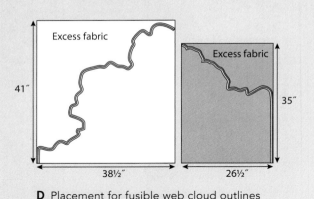

D Placement for fusible web cloud outlines

6 Prepare the sky and cloud fabrics:

> **a.** Cut the light blue fabric into a piece 40″ × 49″. Cut the remaining fabric into 2 pieces 17½″ × 24¾″. Sew the 2 smaller pieces together along the 17½″ sides, and then sew the resulting piece to the 40″ × 49″ piece along the longer sides. You should have a 49″ × 57″ sky piece. The area with more seams will be the bottom of the sky. **FIGURE C**

> **b.** Cut the white fabric to 38½″ × 41″.

> **c.** Cut the light gray fabric to 26½″ × 35″.

7 Prepare the cloud appliqués (pages PDF11-1–PDF11-14). Note that these patterns consist of single lines, not enclosed shapes. Trace the lines onto the fusible web and cut out, leaving a ½″ margin on either side of the lines. Fuse the web to the wrong side of the light gray and white fabrics as indicated. **FIGURE D**

Note which side of the line is the appliqué and which is excess fabric. Cut out each cloud appliqué by trimming on the original marked line.

8 Place the gray cloud appliqué on top of the light blue rectangle, lining up the right and bottom edges. Fuse in place. **FIGURE E**

9 Place the white cloud appliqué on top of these 2 pieces, lining up the left and bottom edges. Fuse in place. **FIGURE F**

10 Stitch the appliqués to the blue background (refer to Fusible Web Appliqué, page 14).

11 To reduce bulk, carefully trim the blue fabric from beneath the clouds to within approximately ½″ of the stitching line, and then trim the gray fabric beneath the white cloud in the same manner.

12 Use the window pattern to help place the beige background piece, right side up, on top of the sky/cloud appliqué, also right side up. Center the sky/cloud within the oval window opening. Fuse in place. Stitch around the opening. To reduce bulk, trim the extra sky/cloud fabric away from behind the beige fabric, ½″ away from the stitching line. **FIGURE G**

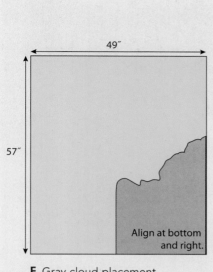

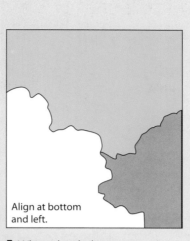

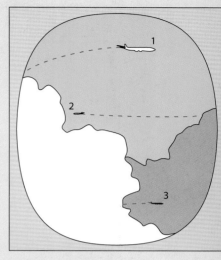

E Gray cloud placement   **F** White cloud placement   **G** Placement diagram

13 Prepare the plane appliqués (page PDF11-33). Following the placement diagram, position and pin the appliqués on the sky and cloud fabrics. **FIGURE G**

14 When you are satisfied with the placement, fuse the plane appliqués in place.

15 Stitch the plane appliqués to the background.

16 If you wish, embroider around all appliqués (refer to Finishing Raw-Edge Appliqué with Embroidery, page 20).

17 Following the placement diagram, mark the red lines behind each plane appliqué with a removable marker. Stitch or embroider along the marked lines with red floss and a backstitch or stem stitch (page 22).

Finishing

For more information about basting, marking, quilting, and binding your quilt, see Finishing the Quilt (page 23).

QUILTING

1 Layer the quilt top, batting, and backing; baste.

2 Quilt as desired.

WHAT I DID

I quilted an allover swirl pattern in the clouds and radiating lines in the blue part of the sky. I filled the beige area around the window with a geometric pattern.

BINDING

1 Trim the batting and backing flush with the quilt top.

2 Refer to Making Bias Binding (page 27) or use your favorite method to make the binding.

3 Bind the quilt.

EEP THIN

PERSPEC

PERSPECTIVE, 70˝ × 54˝, made by Casey York, quilted by Angela Walters, 2013

PERSPECTIVE

FINISHED SIZE: 70″ × 54″

I love using type in quilts, so I am particularly fond of alphabet patterns. This alphabet uses the appearance of shadow and negative space to indicate the letters. The entire alphabet is included in the pattern so you can create your own message.

materials

Unless otherwise noted, all measurements refer to 40″-wide, 100% cotton quilting fabric. Measurements given are for the quilt shown.

WHITE PREMIUM MUSLIN: 1¾ yards 90″ or wider for background, or 3⅛ yards for pieced background

DARK GRAY: approximately 6″ × 6″ piece per letter, or ⅔ yard for phrase as shown

BACKING: 4½ yards

BATTING: 62″ × 78″

BINDING: ⅔ yard for straight-grain binding or 1 yard for bias binding

LIGHTWEIGHT FUSIBLE WEB, 15″ WIDE: 1½ yards (2–5 letters, depending on width, per ⅛ yard)

EMBROIDERY FLOSS (optional): 2 skeins to match appliqué fabric

Assembling the Quilt Top

Refer to Appliqué Basics (pages 13–22) for details about printing the patterns and using the techniques needed for this project. *The appliqué patterns do not require any seam allowance. Use a ¼″ seam allowance for piecing, unless otherwise stated.*

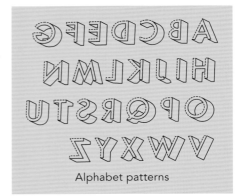
Alphabet patterns

1 Choose a word or phrase to appliqué, and print the corresponding letters from the *Perspective* alphabet patterns (page PDF12-1–PDF12-10). You need to print only a single copy of each letter required, but you'll need to trace as many multiples as you need onto fusible web. Fuse to the wrong side of appliqué fabric. When the patterns are fused to the appliqué fabric, do *not* cut out the appliqués. You will do this as you place them on the background in Step 5.

TIP As you trace the patterns onto the fusible web, label each piece with the letter to which it belongs. When you cut out the individual pieces, they will look unfamiliar, so I recommend cutting out and placing one letter at a time.

2 Cut or piece background fabric to measure 70″ × 54″.

3 Fold the background fabric in half vertically; press to crease.

4 If you chose a different phrase than I did, use the paper print-outs of the alphabet patterns to roughly determine the layout of your phrase. You may need 1, 2, or 3 lines of text, depending on the phrase. Each line of text will be 4″ high, and I spaced my lines so that there are 3″ between lines. Refer to Marking Guidelines (page 101) for exact directions.

MARKING GUIDELINES

■ For a single line of text, fold the background in half horizontally and press to crease. Measure down from this crease 2″ and mark a horizontal line—this is the baseline for your text.

■ For 2 lines of text, fold the background in half horizontally, but do not press. Along the folded edge, fold the fabric again 1½″ and press. This will create 2 creases in the fabric that are spaced 3″ apart. Unfold the fabric and choose which side will be the upper edge of the quilt. The crease closest to this side is the guideline for the base of the first line of text—line up the lower edges of the appliqués with it. For the second line of text, line up the top edge of each appliqué with the second crease. The result will be 2 evenly spaced lines of text that are 3″ apart.
FIGURES A, B, & C

■ For 3 lines of text, fold the background fabric in half and press to crease. Measure and mark a horizontal line 5″ up—this is the baseline for the first line of text. Measure and mark a horizontal line 2″ down from the crease—this is the baseline for the middle line of text. Measure and mark a third horizontal line 7″ down from the second baseline—this is the baseline for your third line of text. **FIGURE D**

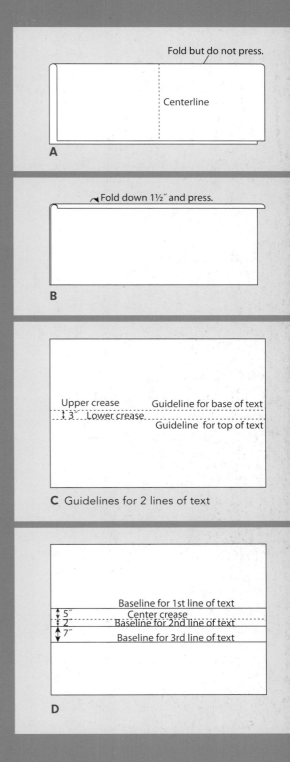

A — Fold but do not press. / Centerline

B — Fold down 1½″ and press.

C — Guidelines for 2 lines of text
Upper crease / Guideline for base of text
3″ Lower crease / Guideline for top of text

D
Baseline for 1st line of text
5″ Center crease
2″ Baseline for 2nd line of text
7″ Baseline for 3rd line of text

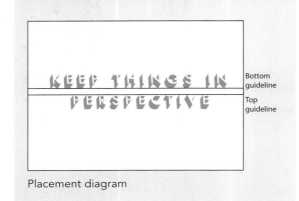

Placement diagram

5 Beginning with the center letters and working toward the right and left edges of the quilt top, arrange the appliqués on the background fabric, cutting out shapes for each letter as you go. You may find it useful to refer to the printouts you made of each letter in order to determine how the appliqué pieces should be placed in relation to each other within each letter. Line up the appropriate edge of each letter with the guideline(s) you made in Step 4.

TIP Pay close attention to the orientation of and spacing between the letters. Use a clear, gridded ruler to place letters parallel to each other and perpendicular to the horizontal guideline, and use consistent spacing between letters. In *Perspective*, I put about 2˝ between letters.

6 When you are satisfied with the placement, fuse the appliqués in place.

7 Stitch the appliqués to the background (refer to Fusible Web Appliqué, page 14).

8 If you wish, embroider around all appliqués (refer to Finishing Raw-Edge Appliqué with Embroidery, page 20).

Finishing

For more information about basting, marking, quilting, and binding your quilt, see Finishing the Quilt (page 23).

QUILTING

1 Layer the quilt top, batting, and backing; baste.

2 You can use the letter patterns to help mark your quilting.

3 Quilt as desired.

WHAT I DID

This quilt is all about negative and empty space. The negative space between the shadows suggests the letter forms, so I had the quilting outline those. I had the empty space surrounding the letters quilted with an abstract geometric pattern that complements the simple sans serif forms of the letters themselves.

BINDING

1 Trim the batting and backing flush with the quilt top.

2 Refer to Making Bias Binding (page 27) or use your favorite method to make the binding.

3 Bind the quilt.

RESOURCES

I wish I could list all of the resources that I used in the writing of this book. Unfortunately, space permits me to name only a few. Here are the ones that I have found most useful for creating the projects and understanding the theory that underlies them.

BOOKS ON PERSPECTIVE IN WESTERN ART

Alberti, Leon Battista. *De Pictura*. 1435–1436. Translated by Rocco Sinisgalli. Cambridge, UK: Cambridge University Press, 2011.

Descargues, Pierre. *Perspective*. Translated by I. Mark Paris. New York: Harry N. Abrams, Inc., 1976.

Gombrich, E. H. *Art and Illusion: A Study in the Psychology of Pictorial Representation*. New York: Pantheon Books, Inc., 1960.

Wright, Lawrence. *Perspective in Perspective*. London: Routledge & Kegan Paul, 1983.

FABRICS

Robert Kaufman Fabrics
robertkaufman.com

Michael Miller Fabrics
michaelmillerfabrics.com

Westminster Fibers/ FreeSpirit Fabrics
westminsterfabrics.com
freespiritfabric.com

Moda Fabrics/United Notions
unitednotions.com

Spoonflower
spoonflower.com

ONLINE SUPPLIERS

Fabric.com
(carries Robert Kaufman's 118˝-wide premium bleached muslin)
fabric.com

Fat Quarter Shop
fatquartershop.com

Pink Chalk Fabrics
pinkchalkfabrics.com

Hawthorne Threads
hawthornethreads.com

Purl Soho
purlsoho.com

Pink Castle Fabrics
pinkcastlefabrics.com

BATTING

The Warm Company
warmcompany.com

THREADS

Aurifil Threads • *www.aurifil.com*

FUSIBLE WEB

Pellon • *pellonprojects.com*

SPRING-TENSION EMBROIDERY HOOPS

Darice • *darice.com*

HERA MARKERS

Clover • *clover-usa.com*

About the Author

Photo by Randall Kahn

Casey York received her formal training in art history before turning to design. She is an avid quilter and designer, drawing her inspiration from masterpieces of the past as well as the contemporary world. Two of her quilts were included in the inaugural QuiltCon quilt show in 2013. Casey has released several stand-alone patterns, and her work has been featured in *Modern Quilts Unlimited* and *Stitch* magazines. She also teaches workshops in embroidery-finished appliqué and improvisational appliqué. She lives in St. Louis with her husband and two sons. To learn more about Casey, please visit her website, casey-york.com, or her blog, studioloblog.wordpress.com.